sweet as the showers of rain

The Bluesmen, Volume II

Samuel Charters

Oak Publications

for Dave Van Ronk

PHOTOGRAPHS

Cover photograph of Bukka White
courtesy of John Fahey

Page 13, Sam Charters
Page 14, Courtesy of the Memphis Public Library
Page 68, Ann Charters
Page 84, Courtesy of Nick Perls
Page 97, Ann Charters
Page 105, Courtesy of George Mitchell
Page 120, Courtesy of Larry Cohen
Page 131, Courtesy of Nick Perls

Copyright © Samuel Charters, 1977
All rights reserved

International Standard Book Number: 0-8256-0178-9
Library of Congress Catalog Card Number: 76-50484

No part of this book may be reproduced or trans-
mitted in any form or by any means, electronic or
mechanical, including photocopying, without permis-
sion in writing from the publisher: Oak Publications, A
Division of Embassy Music Corporation, 33 West 60th
Street, New York 10023

Music Sales Limited
78 Newman Street, London W1, England

Music Sales (Pty) Limited
27 Clarendon Street, Artarmon, Sydney, NSW, Australia

Music Sales Corporation
4-26-22, Jingumae, Shibuya-ku
Tokyo 150, Japan

Cover design by Iris Weinstein

ALSO BY SAMUEL CHARTERS

Poetry
The Children
The Landscape at Bolinas
Poems in an Imagist Manner
Heroes of the Prize Ring
Days
To This Place
From a London Notebook
From a Swedish Notebook
In Lagos

Criticism
Some Poems/Poets

Translations
Baltics
(from the Swedish of Tomas Tranströmer)
We Women
(from the Swedish of Edith Södergran)

Music
Jazz: New Orleans
The Country Blues
The Poetry of the Blues
Jazz: A History of the New York Scene
The Bluesmen
Robert Johnson
The Legacy of the Blues

Contents

Introduction

This is the second and last volume in a study of the regional blues styles before World War II. I had intended to go on and complete a third volume dealing with the rise of the commercial blues in the late thirties and the urban blues of the postwar period, but the commercial blues industry of the Chicago area involves a different approach to the music and becomes involved in larger problems of urban sociology. Also, there has been a great deal written about Chicago's blues after 1945, and Mike Rowe's detailed study, *The Chicago Breakdown*, certainly covers every aspect of the city's musicians and their recording activities. Again, as in the introduction to the first volume, I must stress how much excellent research work is being done by a number of people everywhere in the South, as well as in the urban ghettos in the North. They are, almost all of them, working without grants or assistance of any kind, patiently digging into community records, interviewing older artists, and assembling material of every kind on the recordings themselves. It has been one of the major research efforts made into the arts in America, even if there is little official recognition for the work that they've done. When I was first doing research in these areas in the early fifties I had the South almost to myself; now there seems to be a researcher in every small town in Georgia, Mississippi, Tennessee, and both Carolinas.

Among the people whose recent work has been useful to me in doing this volume, I would like to mention Bruce Bastin for his work in the Greenville, South Carolina, and Durham, North Carolina, areas. Bengt Olsson has been interviewing and searching for older musicians in the Memphis area. George Mitchell supplied me with information from Atlanta when he was working in that area. All of us, of course, are indebted to the blues discographers John Godrich and Robert M. W. Dixon for their *Blues and Gospel Records: 1902-1942* and to the late Mike Leadbitter and Neil Slaven for their *Blues Records: 1943-1966*. Godrich and Dixon also have written a valuable book, *Recording the Blues*, which, although brief, does give some picture of the blues recording industry in the early period. Bastin's material has been gathered into the book

Crying for the Carolinas. Also of particular value for me in this volume has been Dan Mahony's monograph *The Columbia 13/14000-D Series*, which is the source for sales figures and release data on these recordings. Mahony's work is so useful that it only makes it more regrettable that we don't have similar monographs on the other major blues series. I have also found much material in album notes and articles from many sources. There is certainly now enough personal and historical material on the blues artists for us to begin the study of the music and the texts on a more analytical level.

The quotes I've used from Bastin's interviews are in his book *Crying for the Carolinas*, and the Bengt Olsson material is from his book *The Memphis Blues*. Mike Seeger's interview with Frank Walker was printed in the Oak book *The Anthology of American Folk Music*.

My own recent work has been in West Africa, among the people who became part of the Afro-American culture in the American South, and I've begun to see and hear the blues in a new perspective. The relationships that seem to be woven into the song forms of the two areas may finally turn out to be one of the blues' most important aspects, though it's still too soon to form any conclusions. The blues itself, in its American setting, is one of the most interesting of this century's new art forms, and we've only begun to trace its dimensions.

Samuel Charters
Saltsjo Boo, Sweden

Top left: Vocalion promotion for
Memphis Minnie.
Top right: Advertisement for Willie
McTell, John Estes and the Memphis
Jug Band.
Bottom right: Advertisement for the
first John Estes recording.

Memphis and the Singers of Tennessee

1.
Memphis and the Singers of Tennessee

There isn't much left to Beale Street now. You walk along the main street in downtown Memphis, and you turn away from the river, down the sloping blocks to what is now called W.C. Handy Park, and before you've gone a hundred yards you realize that the next time you walk down Beale Street it may not be there at all. It's been many years since Beale was the wide-open, roaring center of bars and honky-tonks that was as well known throughout America as New Orleans' Basin Street—but the buildings were still there. You could stand on a corner and look at the old brick facades, at the old high windows with dirty shades still pulled down late in the afternoon. A whole section of Beale had been taken over by pawnshops and cheap variety stores, but they had a ragged charm of their own, and you could still see blues and gospel records tacked up in some of the window displays. Further on, past the park, there were still some of the old pool halls and barbershops that had been part of the street's life. And beyond them you could walk along the lines of crumbling mansions that once had a more colorful history.

But now, a block down Beale Street, you begin to pass boarded-up store fronts, the elegant nineteenth century brickwork fronts behind the peeling plywood looking as though they're standing on their toes, trying to see over the obstruction. Beyond Handy Park there are only gaping openings where buildings once stood, and the corner where you might still have heard a struggling bluesman or a ragged street band is now the green boundary of a freeway. First Prohibition came to Beale Street, then reform politics, and finally urban renewal. Now there isn't much left except a name on some old records, the title of a blues song, and Handy Park, which seems just an extension of the ground beside the freeway since it's become a park without people. There are not even many old men who still remember it, except as something as dim and unlikely as their own childhood.

Nearly every Southern city was a center for some kind of blues—except maybe

Richmond or New Orleans, which were too close to the edges of the South. But of all these cities, Memphis emerged as one of the most important centers of the blues. Part of the reason was the city's importance as a center of business and industry on the Mississippi River. It sprawls behind mud bluffs along the river's edge more than 400 miles north of New Orleans and more than 300 miles south of St. Louis. It's the largest city on the river between the two. It was always known as a cotton center, but it's also an important market for timber. It has a cluster of railroads feeding into it, and there's endless shipping making its way up and down the Mississippi's muddy current. It has a population now of about a half million, of whom about a third are black, and it was a large city even in the period when Beale Street was booming.

Even more than its general personality as a trade center and a river town, Memphis was a center for music because it was close to the farms and the back country of the Mississippi Delta, which opens out about fifteen miles south of the city. It was in the Delta that the blues first began, and most of the Delta bluesmen came in and out of Memphis at one time or another. With a whole blues culture close to it—and the barrooms and honky-tonks of Beale Street to give the singers a place to gather—Memphis for years had an incredibly rich musical life, and because of the activities of the record companies who visited it regularly much of the music found its way onto records.

But Memphis is even better known for its own blues style than for the Mississippi blues that was also there. Memphis had its jug bands: small street groups using guitar and harmonica, a jug and a banjo, to accompany the blues and the country dance songs found everywhere along Beale Street. The two best known groups were the Memphis Jug Band and Cannon's Jug Stompers, but there were others who also got onto records—as well as ones that played for only a month or two along Beale Street and then drifted back to the countryside. It was the jug bands, whose music was mixed with the blues, that gave the city's music much of its style; but its bluesmen as well, including Furry Lewis, Frank Stokes, and Jim Jackson, added to the burst of sound that could be heard any night along the sidewalks of Beale Street.

Because of the range of Memphis music it is difficult to make any stylistic generalizations. The singing was usually rather straight and simple, without melismatic embellishment and with the melody tones clearly enunciated, as in much of the singing in northern Mississippi. There was a sophisticated approach to older material, so the harmonic range was larger than in much of the Delta blues, though the vocal scale tended to group itself around the blues modes using a flatted third and seventh. Often, as with Furry Lewis and Will Shade and other singers from the Memphis Jug Band, the singing had almost an amateurish hesitancy about pitch and phrasing, but this only enhanced the loose and informal feeling of Memphis music.

It's fortunate that most of the important recording in Memphis was done by one of the most brilliant artist and repertory directors working in the South in the twenties, Ralph Peer of Victor. Peer was from a middle-class background—his father owned a record store in Kansas City—and he had two years at North-western University before starting with the Columbia Phonograph Company of Kansas City in 1911. In 1919 he came to New York as director of production with General Phonograph Corporation, but the next year he became recording director for their subsidiary, OKeh Records. With OKeh he began the first "race" series, and in fact invented the name used to describe black material in the period. With OKeh he recorded the first blues record, Mamie Smith's "That Thing Called Love," early in 1920, and he went on to record a wide range of black music, both blues and jazz—including some country artists like Sylvester Weaver. As early as 1923 he traveled to Atlanta with a portable unit to record white country music there. He recorded the fiddler Fiddlin' John Carson, and then went on and recorded black singers working in the city, among them Lucille Bogan and Fannie Goosby. It was the first field trip by any of the companies, and it set a pattern that Peer was to continue for several years, traveling regularly to Atlanta, where the wholesale distributor Polk Brockman was scouting for him, to New Orleans, and to St. Louis, where a local record shop owner named Jesse Johnson was the scout. In St. Louis he found Lonnie Johnson and with him had one of the most successful of the male blues artists.

Late in 1926 OKeh became part of the American Recording Corporation's group of labels and in effect became a subsidiary of Columbia Records. Peer would have become part of a larger artist and repertory staff under the direction of one of his most serious competitors, Frank Walker. Instead, he left and went to Victor Records, which had been struggling for years to establish a blues line. At the same time Peer had begun to realize the potential in song copyrights, and in 1928 he and Victor established, together, the Southern Music Publishing Company. Peer almost immediately began working in Memphis, probably because no one else had to any extent, and he realized that if he wanted to establish a blues catalog he would have to find artists in areas where no one had looked before.

Of all the important artist and repertory directors working in the South, Peer was the one best suited to Memphis and its musicians. He didn't have the best ear for the sudden, large selling records—Mayo Williams at Vocalion was the most successful at that; and he didn't have Frank Walker's rougher hand with country artists. But he had a sensitive and intelligent ear, and perhaps because he was concerned with the songs themselves, as well as with the artists, he seemed to bring out depths in his artists that other people recording weren't able to get. The range of artists that he worked with was very wide, and the Memphis music, with its distinctive shadings and its quiet lyricism, fit into his careful approach. In a publicity release by Southern Music, published some years after Peer's death, there was an effort to list Peer's artists.

> It is well known that Peer discovered and recorded the legendary Jimmie Rodgers, father of the country field, as well as the legendary Carter Family. It is not so well-remembered that he recorded many other notables in the country, blues, gospel, and jazz categories. These include Ernest Stoneman, Rabbit Brown, Sleepy John Estes, Blind Willie McTell, Frank Stokes, Luke Jordan, Furry Lewis, Bennie

*Moten, Jelly Roll Morton, Fats Waller, Cannon's Jug Stompers, the
Memphis Jug Band (Will Shade), the Dixieland Jug Blowers (Clifford
Hayes), Noah Lewis, Jim Jackson, Jimmie Davis, the McGravy Broth-
ers and the Carolina Tar Heels. Too, he recorded the great blues sing-
er, Mamie Smith, in her first recording, "That Thing Called Love,"
on OKeh.*

Largely because of his activity in the city we have an unparalleled glimpse of
the musical activity in Memphis in the late twenties.

Beale Street is gone now, but the old neighborhoods north of the town center
still have their rows of one-story wood houses behind straggling patches of grass
and the uneven sidewalks under the spindly trees. Children play in the water-
filled gutters after a rainstorm, and old men gather to talk on benches beside
the grocery stores. Along one of the streets, if you know which grocery store
to look for, you can find Bukka White sitting on one of the old chairs he's put
out as his "office." Along another, if you know which weathered door to try,
you can find Furry Lewis sitting beside his bed, his guitar on the wall, as he
smokes a cigarette and looks quietly out at the houses across the street. The
blues is still living in Memphis, even if the buildings that nursed it have been
destroyed to make way for a future that perhaps will have forgotten that the
blues was once there.

Beale Street today.

13

The only known photo of the Memphis Jug Band: (left to right) Ben Ramey, Will Shade, Charlie Polk, and Will Weldon.

2.
The
Memphis Jug Band

What people seem to remember most about Beale Street is its looseness—its lack of fuss and pretense. It was a wide-open neighborhood with a lot of music in the clubs or on the street itself, a lot of casual drinking, and a lot of sex that didn't cost much money. Memphis itself wasn't a formal town. It was still part of the surrounding country, a place where people growing cotton came in to do business, go out to a restaurant, stay over in a hotel, then go back out to their farms. It wasn't Chicago or New York—not even Atlanta or New Orleans. Loose —easy without much sophistication, but open and responsive to everything. The music of the Memphis Jug Band, perhaps the most typical of all the city's groups that recorded, had a little of all of these factors in its music, and in their way they reflected their surroundings as much as the Delta singers reflected theirs. It was part of the blues they did, with some of the casual drifting sound of men just in town for a long Saturday night—it was part of their minstrel songs, songs they played for Memphis whites—it was part of the classic blues they did with Hattie Hart, sounding a little like the Chicago recordings of Ma Rainey and her Tub Jug Orchestra—it was part of the folk songs and comedy songs they did when they went off in the picking season as part of the traveling medicine shows.

The Memphis Jug Band was part of Beale Street, and it seemed to reflect its rows of garish saloons and shabby stores, the dirty streets in back of it with their crumbling mansions and peeling wood boarding houses. Their music often had a rumpled sound to it, as though they were tucking in their shirttails as they played. Then at other times, other sessions, when somebody had a new song or a new arrangement, it all came together with a sudden smoothness, almost an elegance. Then on a session the next day they'd begin a song with a kind of one-by-one uncertainty, get confused in the instrumental choruses, then have to rely on their shouted enthusiasm to get them through the piece. This is what Beale Street was by this time—and this was Beale Street's music, the music of its jug bands.

15

The Memphis Jug Band was almost this loose and casual about its music, despite the players' seriousness and their complete involvement in what they were doing. Their sincerity, their complete honesty about the music came, as much as anything else, from the man who was responsible for the band, an open, warm singer and harmonica player named Will Shade—though he was always called Son by everybody in the band, since he'd been raised by a woman named Annie Brimmer and called Son Brimmer by the neighbors. He was still part of Beale Street and the jug band until his death in the 1960s. He lived in a crumbling tenement off an alley behind Beale, with a guitar under his bed and his harmonica shoved into a pocket and a book with painfully jotted phone numbers of the musicians around that he could still count on to come for a party or a session.

Son's band was the first jug band to record in Memphis, but it wasn't the first jug band to record. Clifford Hayes had started to record for Ralph Peer in the early twenties with his Louisville jug bands on OKeh, and with the name the Dixieland Jug Blowers they'd been very successful on Victor. They'd even added the great New Orleans clarinetist Johnny Dodds for one session, and one of the pieces—called, for no reason in particular, "Memphis Shake"—was put on the other side of a brilliant band release by Jelly Roll Morton and the Red Hot Peppers. But Son's music wasn't like the disciplined jazz of the Hayes group. His music was blues and country minstrel songs, and this is what his band played—with their own warmth and loose excitement.

Son was one of the few Memphis musicians who was born there (on February 5, 1898) and he grew up as one of the crowd of small boys who hung around the fringes of Beale Street. He played more harmonica with the jug band than he did guitar, but the guitar was his first instrument. He remembered learning enough to get started when he was still in his teens. He followed a singer named Tee-Wee Blackman around on the streets, watching his fingers when he played. The first song he learned from him was "Newport News Blues," a blues about the troops leaving Newport News, Virginia, for France in the First World War. Tee-Wee showed him enough so he could play in the key of A and the key of E, and he decided he didn't need any more lessons, but he couldn't figure out any other keys by himself and he had to go back to Tee-Wee again. By the time he'd reached his early twenties he was going down into Mississippi with the medicine shows, and he was singing with a small, young, pretty girl named Jennie Mae Clayton who was living with him just off Beale Street. It was from the two of them and the music they were doing that the Memphis Jug Band had it start.

From an earlier account discussed in *The Country Blues* of their first recording session:

> *When Son came in from a show in 1926, he and Jennie started playing and singing in the bars along Beale Street. One night a man named "Roundhouse" came up to them and asked if he could join their band. Son said it was alright and Roundhouse started blowing*

on a bottle. Everybody at the bar started shouting, "Jug Band! Jug Band!" and they went along the street from bar to bar shouting and laughing. The next day Son decided to get up a band ". . . something like the boys in Louisville." He was talking about . . . the Dixieland Jug Blowers. He got a friend, Ben Ramey, to play kazoo, and another, Charlie Polk, to play jug. (The jug isn't actually played as a musical instrument. The player makes a buzzing sound with his lips and holds the jug up close to his mouth. The jug acts as a resonator for the sound.) They were both young, about Son's age, with more enthusiasm than experience. Son played harmonica or guitar, so they needed a second guitar player. They talked an older, more experienced musician, Will Weldon, into joining them and they started playing along the street. Charlie Williamson, at the Palace, heard them and got them an audition with Ralph Peer. Peer came down to the theatre on Saturday morning and they played for him on the stage. He liked them and told them to have four blues ready for him when he got back from a recording trip to New Orleans.

On February 24, 1927, they made their first recording for Victor. They had been up all night rehearsing, but after a little to drink, Peer got them relaxed enough to play. In the middle of their second song Williamson came into the studio to hear how they were doing. Son remembers that Charlie was always a fancy dresser and that morning he had on a gray suit, gray spats, a green paisley waistcoat and a white derby. Charlie strolled in, took off his derby and put it down on the piano. There was a hollow bang when he put it down and Son was sure the test was ruined. He looked at the control room window and Peer was standing there laughing at the whole scene.

They did four blues in their morning session, with Will Weldon singing the first two, "Son Brimmer Blues" and "Stingy Woman Blues." Charlie Polk —whose jug was almost inaudible anyway—sang the lead on the third song, "Memphis Jug Blues," with Will and Son singing harmony. Son had moved from harmonica to guitar and the two guitars had a string band flavor, with one of them capoed up high like a tenor guitar. Son sang his old "Newport News Blues" for the fourth song. The beginnings were ragged on their songs—usually Son starting it off, then Weldon coming in a beat or two later, and finally Ben and Charlie. But once they all got started the band had a good beat and the instrumental sound was strong. Ben could play almost cornetlike choruses on the kazoo, and Son's harp playing had a soft wistful charm. The singing was tight and nervous—Will didn't have any of the assurance he was to develop years later as the successful Vocalion artist Casey Bill, and Son was always more of an instrumentalist than a singer, but the harmony was good on "Memphis Jug Blues," and some of the best things they recorded later used vocal harmonies. Despite the nervousness of all of it— they were all young and unsure about what they were doing—the records had a kind of friendly appeal to them. Peer seems to have been satisfied enough to offer Son a contract and to bring the band up to Chicago to record four months later, on June 9, 1927.

Their Chicago trip was one of their few stays outside of Memphis, and it was also one of their most exotic brushes with success. They had decided to bring another harmonica player up with them so Son could play guitar, and they used a friend—a tall, thin musician called Shakey Walter. It was after this session that they had an offer to play at the Grand Central Theatre in Chicago with the Butterbeans and Susie review. Butterbeans and Susie were a blues duet team whose real names were Joe and Susie Edwards. They did some singing and some comedy and added acts like the Memphis Jug Band for variety. As Son remembered it in *The Country Blues*, their life in the theater was short but exciting.

> They decided to do a jungle act with everybody in jungle costumes and Shakey Walter holding a large rattlesnake. They got the snake and pulled its fangs, but when they were having a dress rehearsal the snake got loose and started for a rat hole in the wall of the auditorium where they were rehearsing. Shakey caught it behind the neck and they finally got it back into its box, but they decided that they'd better not feed it so much so it wouldn't have the strength to wiggle. They opened at the Grand on Monday, June 20, 1927, wearing grass skirts and playing their guitars. Shakey and a girl from the chorus took turns holding the snake and singing. Son sang "Newport News" and they played some instrumental numbers and the audience seemed to like it very much. Ma Rainey heard about the act and booked them into Gary, Indiana, for her show the next week.
>
> At Gary the act came to a disastrous close. One of Ma's chorus girls was from the country and she felt sorry for the snake because nobody was feeding it. She gave it some food without bothering to tell anybody. In the middle of the show the revived snake began inching out of the hand of the little chorus girl who was dancing with it. It finally got its head free enough to turn around and nip her. It didn't have any fangs, but it had small teeth, and she screamed and let go. The snake immediately started for the footlights, since everybody was on stage, and the theatre panicked. The first ten rows of the audience climbed over the back of the seats, the orchestra scrambled under the stage, and Ma, fat as she was, jumped on top of the grand piano. Shakey made a dive for the snake and got it just as it was going into the orchestra pit. He scrambled to his feet, waving the snake, pretending to talk to it in a nonsense dialect. He started to dance around the stage with it and Son finally came to enough to start playing. After a moment of hesitation the audience gingerly started back to the seats and finally decided it was all part of the act. They got a rousing ovation. From Ma, herself, they got considerably less than an ovation. "If you bring that——snake on this stage again I'll have everyone of you put in jajl." Without the snake their act wasn't very exciting and they went back to Memphis.

They didn't have a lot of jobs in Memphis; there was a little scene around

Beale Street and the clubs but not enough. So they scuffled up whatever they could. An agent named Howard Yancey was getting them jobs for country dances and the kind of white society jobs that black groups could get in the South. They were mostly expected to play familiar songs for dancing, to get drunk and act foolish, and to look grateful for getting the job. They came in and went out the same door as the kitchen help, and whatever eating and drinking they did was back in the kitchen. The jug band did a lot of these jobs in Memphis, some of them at the Chickasaw Country Club, others in the Peabody Hotel, where they played for businessmen's stag parties. The tips were good, even if the jobs were unpleasant, and if they played at a party for somebody like Mayor Crump they got ten dollars apiece before the job started. The clubs on Beale Street were noisy and crowded, and most people in them were there to drink or gamble or look for women; in all the confusion and the casual drifting there wasn't any way for a country jug band to cause much of a stir.

They had recorded blues in Chicago, but they'd also recorded a swaggering version of the old English folk song "Bully of the Town," starting with a Charleston chorus for kazoo, two guitars, and jug. The vocal was a haphazard unison chorus with everybody singing as much of the words as they knew, and there were instrumental "jazz" breaks for kazoo and jug. Shakey Walter was a fine harp player, and he was very strong in the instrumental chorus of the "Sunshine Blues" that was recorded at the same session. They were selling enough records for Victor to do a little advertising. An ad in the Memphis newspapers showed a picture of the band. Son and Will Weldon were sitting in front with their guitars, Son grinning broadly. Ben Ramey was behind Son's shoulder, wearing a coat and tie, holding a long kazoo in his hand. Charlie Polk was in a jacket, a button sweater, and a shirt with a loose, open collar, holding a large earthenware jug and smiling almost to himself. A drawing made from the photograph—putting neckties on all of them and buttoning Charlie's collar— was used in the advertisements for the *Chicago Defender*.

Peer only waited until the end of the summer, then he brought them to Atlanta to record again. They did two sessions—on October 19 and 20, 1927. There were changes in the band for the six pieces they recorded. Charlie Polk didn't make the trip, and Son had added Vol Stevens to the band. Vol was born outside of town, but like the others he'd grown up in Memphis; he was living with his sister on Springdale when they were playing together. He played banjo/mandolin and sang. For this trip Son also brought along Jennie Mae, and she sang three blues, "I Packed My Suitcase, Started to the Train," "State of Tennessee Blues," and "Bob Lee Junior Blues." They finished the first session with the popular "Kansas City Blues," then did two songs the next day with Vol Stevens singing "Beale Street Mess Around" and "I'll See You in the Spring, When the Birds Begin to Sing." Vol used a six-string banjo for his own songs, and the rhythm had some of the surging swing of the Louisville bands which also used six-string banjos. Jennie Mae didn't sing again with the band for recording; she sounded very girlish and nervous on her songs, but she had a special quality of her own that added to the band's sound. The words to the songs were stronger in these sessions as well. The texts had been generally put together out of familiar verses, but Vol could put together verses in a stronger sequence, and in one of the first day's songs there was a verse that hasn't turned up in many other blues:

I got a voice like a radio, it broadcasts it everywhere,
I got a voice like a radio, it broadcasts it everywhere,
Now you can find a wild woman, boy, by broadcastin' in the air.

"I'll See You In the Spring" was another folk song, with a chorus that ended:

I'll see you in the spring,
When the birds begin to sing,
It's fare thee, honey, fare you well.

It's always hard to look back and remember something. Years slide into each other, days stretch and dwindle, hours stay in the memory, and whole months—at the same time—have gone completely. Even when the face, the sound of the voice are clearly there it's sometimes impossible to remember when the person first came through a door, or walked down a street. For Son, trying to remember all the musicians who were in and out of the Memphis Jug Band over the years was a long and difficult job. He sat in his shabby room looking down at his hands, drinking cheap wine as he thought back. There was one man he was trying to remember—it was Charlie Burse, who was sitting in the room with him, a thin, well-dressed man with a pencil moustache and a worried expression. They couldn't remember when they'd first met—only that it had been sometime after the Atlanta sessions in October 1927. Finally, as the afternoon got later and the gray winter rain slackened outside the window, he decided that he must have met Charlie before the next sessions, in Memphis three and a half months later. He knew that they'd met one night when he had a session coming up the next morning in the McCall Building Studio. In a club on Beale Street, Yardbird's, he heard a man entertaining in the back room, singing and playing a four-string tenor guitar. The man had on flashy clothes and he laughed as he sang, and he often called himself Laughing Charlie. He was a country musician just in from Decatur, Alabama, and he had a whole repertoire of the kind of songs you could hear at county fairs or farm auctions.

Charlie and Son became close friends, and they were friends until they died within a few months of each other. They both remembered that they had met that way, but they couldn't remember just when it could have been. The band did six songs in February 1928, but Charlie wasn't with them. He didn't do his first recording with them until the next fall, on September 11. But the sessions in February showed already how far the band had come in only a year. They had a style, a sense of professionalism. The songs started with a rush and kept up their excitement. There were little musical figures worked out in the arrangements, and the singing—even if it wasn't on a level with the greatest singers of the twenties—was strong and musical. The band that Charlie came into was a tight musical group, with a uniqueness and raw musicality in everything they did. Charlie himself added a last dimension—a noisy, uninhibited country dance rhythm, some new songs, and his irrepressible laugh. The engineers had trouble recording him—he tapped his foot too loud, so they put him up on a high stool, but he kicked the legs of that too. They finally had to put a pillow under his feet to keep the noise down.

As far as Victor Records and Ralph Peer were concerned, the Memphis Jug Band—with whatever musicians Son brought to the studio—was a successful recording act, and Son was early put on a royalty advance basis. For nearly four years he was paid $25 a week, which was a reasonable sum for the 1920s, and he was expected to arrange the sessions, write the tunes or use tunes that someone else in the band had written, and take care of rehearsals. Son took the job seriously, and he was always ready when the Victor recording unit was in Memphis, even if they didn't record the band on every trip. When the band was in the studio they were paid $50 for each side they recorded, and they split the money up among themselves. For their usual four blues sessions they got a total of $200 advance. Son had composer royalties, and they could go as high as six cents a record if he'd written the songs on both sides; even higher royalty rates were paid if there were sales in Europe or Canada. Between the royalties, the session advances, and the band's jobs, Son had more money than he needed for everyday expenses; so Peer talked him into buying some Victor common stock, and Son and Jennie Mae bought a house in Memphis.

As the band became more professional they were also useful to Peer in other sessions, as he could expect Son to get something together with the other musicians. They were behind a number of lead singers, from Memphis Minnie, who had just started recording when she did "Bumble Bee Blues " and "Meningitis Blues" with them in May 1930, to Hattie Hart and Charlie "Bozo" Nickerson. Hattie Hart was a Memphis woman who sang in the style of the popular New York blues artist Sara Martin, and she had a heavily dramatic style that didn't fit comfortably into the band's informality. Charlie Nickerson was a piano player and entertainer from the "Steamboat Bill from Louisville" show, touring black theaters in the South, and he recorded a vaudeville-flavored "Everybody's Talkin' about Sadie Green" in another May 1930 session. Son and one of his close friends, a piano player named Edward Hatchett who was playing at the Midway at 4th and Beale, accompanied another friend, Kaiser Clifton, when he did four blues at still another session in May 1930. Son even played guitar and harmonica for a religious group, the Memphis Sanctified Singers.

Peer usually wrote ahead to Son and gave him about two months to get ready for a recording date. The band always worked at Son's house, and they'd work all day on a song, going over and over it ten or fifteen times until they had it right. Son never was insistent on a hard, tight arrangement, but he knew how he wanted the arrangements to go, and he stayed with a song until they had worked something out that he liked. Jennie Mae would write down the words and when they'd played it and timed it Son would write his "OK" on the words; then he'd write in the title at the top and his name on the bottom so that Peer's Southern Music Corporation could copyright it. He tried to be as careful as he could with the copyrights, and nearly thirty years later, when I was able to write Southern Music and tell them I'd found Son living in Memphis, they were able to renew all of his copyrights. At the same time they sent him an advance on what they hoped might be some further earnings.

In the last year of the Victor contract, 1930, Peer had the Memphis Jug Band in the studio for nine different sessions, and in that year alone they recorded twenty titles. There was so much material that some of the things recorded late in the year were released under other names—like the Memphis Sheiks or the Carolina Peanut Boys—or under Charlie Nickerson's name. There were fifty-seven songs recorded for Victor over the four years of the contract, and Son used fourteen or fifteen different musicians, from his old guitar teacher, Tee-Wee Blackman, who played with them on their fine train blues "K.C. Moan," to friends like Hambone Lewis and Jab Jones, who played jug on different sessions. There were so many different people singing that it's difficult to say that any kind of blues was typical of the Memphis Jug Band. They even recorded two instrumental waltzes, "Jug Band Waltz" and "Mississippi River Waltz," in September 1928.

The financial crash of the early thirties ended Victor's recording activities in Memphis, even if it didn't end the Memphis Jug Band. The last sessions, in November 1930, had to be done in a banquet room at the Peabody Hotel, since the old studio in the McCall Building had been closed up. Peer settled accounts with Son, and he said goodbye to all of them as they left the studio. Son had managed to buy nearly $3000 worth of Victor stock with his royalties, but he had to sell it at a fraction of its face value and he and Jennie Mae had to give up the house. He kept struggling to keep the band going. They went to Chicago in 1932 and managed to get a session with Champion at their studios in Richmond, Indiana. Vol Stevens and Will Weldon were on the trip, and Jab Jones was on piano now—playing jug only some of the time. Otto Gilmore played drums. They did five songs that were released under various names, among them the Picaninny Jug Band and the Jolly Jug Band. They were in Chicago again on November 6, 7, and 8, 1934, with a slightly different band. Vol Stevens had been replaced by a violinist, Charlie Pierce, and Charlie Burse's brother, Robert, on washboard, had replaced the drummer. They managed to get three days of recording with OKeh, and they did twenty sides, the last releases by the Memphis Jug Band.

The sound in 1934 was different from the things they'd recorded for Ralph Peer. There were none of the gentle folk blues like "K.C. Moan" or "Stealin' Stealin'." With the washboard and Jab Jones's rolling piano style they were more of a country skiffle group, and there were more instrumentals and a jazz feeling to a lot of the solos. Son played fine harmonica and Robert Burse had a wide range of objects to hit on his washboard, including a large orchestra cymbal that he used on "Gator Wobble." They did wild, exciting versions of songs like "Take Your Fingers Off it" and "Boodie Bum Bum," with verses like:

Oh, the black cat told the white one,
let's go 'cross town and clown.
I said the black cat told the white one,
let's go 'cross town and clown.
And that white cat told the black one,
you better set your black self down.

It was exuberant, rough music. Most of the pieces were issued first on OKeh and then later on Vocalion, but nothing was selling much in 1934 and Son couldn't keep it going. Charlie Burse had two sessions in 1939, recording twenty titles with a larger swing-type group called Charlie Burse and his Memphis Mudcats that used a conventional piano, bass, and drums rhythm section. The days of the jug band were over.

The Depression had finished off what was left of Beale Street, and the years drifted by. There were odd jobs at the country club and at the homes of some of the white society people. Whoever got a job would call up people to get them to come play too. Laura Dukes—known as "Little Bit"—a close friend of Son and Jennie Mae, played the ukelele or ukelele banjo and did a lot of singing. Will Batts, a violinist, ran a band that included Milton Robie who'd once been in the jug band, and usually Laura Dukes and Robert Burse, and for parties there were other musicians always ready, including Son and Charlie. The jobs were usually an hour's entertaining—most of the time in a side room, while a dance orchestra played for the social side of things in the main room. They were a kind of souvenir of the old South, and as always there was a lot of drinking and a lot of clowning. A white man named Jim Strainer was often responsible for getting them home, and the jug band did a blues for him, "Jim Strainer's Blues."

But as the years went by there were fewer people interested in what they were doing. Charlie had always been a house painter, and he just went back to his regular job. Will Batts kept his band going until 1956, when he died of a stroke. Son had even learned to play the string bass a little and he was working with the band as well. Howard Yancey booked a lot of the jobs for the musicians—though Will Batts did his own bookings—and a woman named Mrs. Wagner used to book them for jobs outside of Memphis.

In November 1956, on a drab, wet morning, I found Howard Yancey still in his old office upstairs at 316 Beale Street. "You interested in those old jug bands? They're still playing." It wasn't much of an office, and times were hard for Yancey, as they were for the musicians. Son was working on and off in a tire-recapping plant—a large, cluttered garage—a few blocks off Beale Street. He'd always had trouble with a strained back from his youth, and with that and his drinking he wouldn't have kept the job except that the man who owned the garage liked his old records. He and Jennie Mae were living in a small, poor room in an unpainted building on Mulberry Street. He was excited to talk about his music and about recording again. He still looked like the man in the old advertisements; he had the same smile, though his face was heavier. He was wearing a sagging sweatshirt and trousers stained from his job. He hadn't seen Gus Cannon for nearly a year, but he had Burse's address, on a small street in South Memphis.

When we went over that evening Charlie was looking at television, but like Son he was excited to talk about music and his newest band. He even had an acetate test of a song that he'd made the summer before with the band—a rhythm and blues group with Son on washtub bass. He said he'd be over at Son's in the morning and they'd try to find Cannon. The next morning all three of them were there. A friend of Son's had seen Gus going into a laundry and he'd told him Son was looking for him. After a few minutes they decided they wanted to record again, and my portable machine was brought in from the car. I didn't have much money left—about 12 dollars—but they split it up and spent some of it for whiskey and a harmonica for Son. Cannon and Burse came back first with a cheap American harmonica, but Son said it wasn't good enough and they finally went back and got him a Hohner "Marine Band," the instrument most of the bluesmen use. For the rest of the afternoon—until the last light had dwindled in the winter afternoon—they sat in Son's room and played. They didn't stop until it was too dark to see the instruments. From the first description of the session in *The Country Blues*:

> . . . At first they were tight and nervous, but Son, despite quite a bit of wine, began to pull the group together, just as he must have done at many recording sessions thirty years before.
>
> It was exciting to feel his influence on these men, who in the world outside of the dingy, cold room were more successful than he had been. It was not his musicianship—he was a limited musician. It was his earnest, deep sincerity. He had never been a great harmonica player and he hadn't had a harmonica in twenty years, but he began with fierce determination, sitting in a low chair, the harmonica almost hidden in his scarred hands. Before the afternoon was over, he and Charlie created the wonderful "Harmonica-Guitar Blues" that was included in the Folkways record of the session. While the others were outside, he played on an old guitar that Cannon had brought until he was able to re-create some of the magnificent blues he had recorded years before.

It wasn't as it had been in the twenties, when there were a dozen musicians to call up, and there were new songs and new ideas to try. There wasn't much music left, but Son still could play as much harp as ever, and he was one of the finest of the country harp players. And he could still sing one of his most poignant blues:

What you going to do, Mama,
When your troubles get like mine.
Take a mouthful of sugar
And drink a bottle of turpentine.
I can't stand it.
I can't stand it.
Drop down, Mama,
Sweet as the showers of rain.

He got an old guitar after that, and he worked a little with Charlie. Milton Robie was still living on College Street and Charlie's brother Robert was still living off Beale, but the others from the band were dead. Son and Charlie were part of a television tribute to W.C. Handy in the spring of 1958, and they kept going with what they could scuffle up. But by 1959 Son wasn't able to work much anymore. He'd gotten a little money from Southern Music, and now he got welfare checks, and there were things like his Christmas job with Charlie. As he said in 1956:

Me and Charlie work up and down the floors at the McCall Building. Every Christmas we play it, you know, for contributions. This year we didn't hardly make more than $12.

Son and Jennie Mae were living in a crumbling wood building in a muddy open space behind Beale. It was a bad building, and the room they had upstairs was open to anybody who was around. Some of the people hanging out in the hallways and on the stairs were drunk, stumbling neighborhood thieves, and late at night Son was sometimes afraid when someone came to see him. Bo Carter had a small house down the alleyway, and he was living in almost the same squalid poverty as Son and Jennie Mae. He sat blind in his darkened room, talking a little whenever Son brought visitors around. It was still possible to use Son to help find musicians, and for a few dollars he'd try to get people over to his room to play. He recorded his "Newport News Blues" again for Decca in the summer of 1960, and there were young musicians like Charlie Musselwhite beginning to hang around for lessons and a chance to talk. But Son wasn't well, there was too much wine, and the poverty was too oppressive to fend off. The last effort I made to get a session together with him in the spring of 1961 wasn't successful. Laura Dukes came up, and for the first time Memphis Willie Borum turned up from his factory job, and Charlie came around with his tenor guitar. But everyone else from the building pressed into the room, too, and there was angry, drunken wrangling almost drowning out the music. Only Memphis Willie, who was sitting on the edge of the bed close to the wall, was able to keep out of it and go on playing. Laura Dukes and Son couldn't get away from the people around them—and the situation finally got so bad that the best thing to do was leave.

Both Charlie and Son died five years later, in 1966. Charlie had gone on working as a house painter, so there hadn't been the desperation of Son's last years, but for both of them their last efforts to play their music were hard and disappointing. Somehow it kept eluding them—the brilliance of the music they'd made thirty years before. But it was all still there, on the phonograph records they'd made, and for both of them, in wry thoughtful moments, it was almost enough to have it to remember.

Advertisement for Gus Cannon.

3. Cannon's Jug Stompers

Sometimes, as the years drifted by, Gus Cannon had the same wry moments as he thought back to the twenties and the brief period of his life when he was making records. Almost in his nineties now, Gus is still a tall, lean, wiry man, and, though his hair is grizzled and thin, his high laugh is as clear and sudden as always, and his eyes still brighten when he remembers those years. "White folk," he says loudly, using his ordinary expression for anybody who's come to talk to him, "we made us some music." He still gets around along Beale Street by himself, in his gold-rimmed glasses, a suit coat and an open shirt, supported by an elaborate stick that he made himself. In 1956, at the rough session at Son's old apartment on Mulberry Street, he was still playing the banjo and jug, though he couldn't do some of the old songs he could still remember. He sat in the chair close to the window and tried things over and over, shaking his head emphatically from side to side as his fingers fumbled with the strings. His biggest number had ended up with his swinging the banjo back and forth as he played, holding it by the fingers of his left hand around the banjo neck. He tried it a little standing in the half-light by the bed, half turned away while he tried to get it right, but his hands didn't have the feel anymore, and he almost dropped the banjo. His fingers have stiffened now, and the banjo sits in its case in his room, but he still can play the jug and talk with the same abrupt enthusiasm.

The long, still years were easier for Cannon—as the other Memphis musicians always called him—than they were for Son and Charlie. For Son the jug band had been the first important thing in his life, and he'd thrown himself into the business of rehearsals and recording and song writing. It was more important to him, for one reason, because he was so much younger. He was only in his late twenties, and he found himself in the hungry years of the Depression without any other skills to get him through. Cannon was forty-four when he started recording, and when the excitement was over he was still living just about the way he'd been living before. His music was from the pre-blues period, and his repertoire—like other musicians the same age, Jim Jackson among them—was a collection of comedy songs, minstrel show songs, instrumental breakdowns, and interminable, usually bawdy, routines of jokes and stories. These were performed with the broadest gestures and mugging—usually in blackface. Some of the expressiveness of Cannon's face must come from those old days. As he sits talking his face changes from the wide grinning pleasure of something he's just remembered to a petulant shake of his head and a deep frown, with the corners of his mouth almost sagging in his unhappiness; then his lips purse in sudden anger and he shakes his head; then without the slightest hesitation his head is thrown back and he is laughing loudly. A moment later he stops talking and glances carefully at you to see what the effect of it all has been.

An important aspect of the life of men like Cannon is that careful glance after a moment of clowning. Cannon addresses most of the people who come to see him as "white folks" because for him the white world has always been a distant, but continually threatening, aspect of his life. Son was an adolescent during the outbreak of racial violence in the Memphis area in the first years of the World War—when southern whites attempted to slow the rush of black field workers to northern cities with a wave of lynchings and beatings—and as an adolescent he was able to minimalize some of the emotional effect of it. Cannon, however, was older, and he'd spent most of his life as a sharecropper, and since he'd already left Mississippi, where he was born, he was the kind of man who was suspect. He has never said if there were specific instances when the antagonism that was always present between the races in the South singled him out as a victim, but the white man has continued to be the same threat to him, despite the "hilarity" of his shrewd blackface performance, despite the grinning face every black man of his generation learned to present to his watching white neighbors.

For the countryside that he came from, and by the standards of the period when he started playing, he was a professional musician—even if it wasn't the kind of full professionalism that we associate with music today. There wasn't enough money for a performer to spend his time singing and playing in the American rural areas—especially in a period when the absence of recordings or radio meant that there was someone who played an instrument and sang in almost every house. All the performers, white and black, lived and worked as part of their small towns or farm areas, and they did their playing when they weren't working their jobs or on their small farms. It was exceptionally talented men like Cannon who were considered "professional" and who brought their own standards to the music they created. It was this quality, as well as the repertoire, that gave the jug band recordings that Cannon did their distinctiveness. His experience and his musicality—and the experience of his old partner Hosea Woods—gave their performances a brilliance and a coherence that much of the country instrumental recording of the period lacked. Even when they were rough, and some of their songs were uncertain, the broad humor kept everything together. Cannon and his group made an important contribution to the picture we have of Southern music of this early period, and their recordings are still some of the most exciting that came out of the wealth of Memphis music in the 1920s.

Of all the Memphis characteristics in Cannon's style, perhaps it's Memphis as a kind of musical crossroads that's most evident. Like many of the other singers he came out of Mississippi, but without any close identification with the Mississippi blues style which developed after he'd left. He was born in northern Mississippi, in Red Banks, on September 12, 1883, working in the fields when he was a small boy on a poor farm. He always liked music—loved it as a boy—and he wanted to learn the banjo, which was still a popular folk instrument at this time. He made his first instrument himself out of a bread pan and a guitar neck. His mother gave him the bread pan, and he put holes through the sides of it to hold the guitar neck. He covered it with a raccoon skin that he scraped thin. The only problem with this kind of head was that there was no way to tighten it since the instrument didn't have the metal frame and drumhead ring of commercial banjos. He remembers that he always traveled with his pockets full of crumpled newspaper, so he could make a fire before he was going to play. He held the banjo over the flames until the skin head was tight enough so it had a banjo "ring" to it.

He started playing when he had his first banjo and, as he remembered in 1956 during the interviews for *The Country Blues:*

> . . . *The music he learned was that of the old dance songs and reels. The first song he learned was the little dance song "Old John Booker You Call That Gone," and he "strummed" it on the banjo. That is, it was played with a syncopated finger-picking, down-stroking and thumb-picking style that is similar to the older banjo frailing style. Then he followed around after one of the men who could really play, Bud Jackson, from Alabama, and he learned to finger-pick a little jig in 6/8 time. Cannon laughed. "When I had them two songs down, you couldn't teach me nothing, 'cause I knew it* all.

He was able to get himself a real banjo after he'd been playing a short time, and when he was fifteen he was already working small dances in the local countryside. He was living in the Delta at this time, and it's possible that he might have recorded then. From *The Country Blues:*

> *About 1901, when he was seventeen or eighteen, he was in Belzoni, Mississippi, a small town between Yazoo City and Clarksdale. Some people came to his cabin and asked him if he wanted to make a record. He didn't even know what they meant. They told him to bring his banjo and they took him into town where a man had a cylinder recording machine. After getting over his nervousness, Gus played a dance song, singing into the crude metal horn. He remembered the picture of the dog looking into the horn, and he thinks it was somebody from the old Victor recording company. He was paid for his playing and went back to his cabin, still wildly excited at having heard himself play. The early catalogs of Victor, Columbia*

and the Berliner gramophone companies do not list anything specifically as by Cannon, but there are cylindrical recordings of banjo songs and dances one of which could be his cylinder. He may have been recorded by a pioneer field collector whose recordings have been lost, but if the material should ever be found, it would be a priceless collection of black country music.

Even today, as an old man, Cannon still gives an impression of energy, of restless movement. He always has some little job going on, something that he's planning to do somewhere. He seems to have moved as much when he was a young man. He worked in the cotton fields up and down the Delta, sometimes on shares, sometimes for somebody else. He was in and out of most of the small towns, and he still kept playing and singing. He got up to Memphis for the first time just before the war, in 1913, and for the first few days he stayed down on the docks watching the stevedores doing their heavy, hot work carrying and lifting back and forth from the river steamers. He found a small job so he could stay in town and tried to take some music lessons from Professor Handy, but Handy couldn't understand the kind of music Cannon played and he couldn't understand the kind of formal music Handy was trying to teach him, so the lessons ended after a few hours.

He still kept moving around after he got to Memphis. He "made a cotton crop" on some land out on the Macon Road, but the land didn't give much, so he went across the Mississippi the next year and worked a crop outside of Chatfield, Arkansas. The next year he went out of the South, for the season, and put in a crop outside of Cairo, Illinois. He didn't like the cold weather, and he went back to Tennessee at the beginning of the winter. By this time he was playing the banjo almost as much as he was farming, so he was traveling most of the summer, even when he'd gotten a little farm started. In 1916 he was working some land outside of Ripley, about forty-five miles northeast of Memphis, on Route 51, the main highway down through the Delta to New Orleans. Ripley was a small town, a straggling section of stores and feed shops, the small farms coming close to the dirt back streets. It was a quiet town, but like every small place in the South during these years it had its own local musicians. The best of them, and now the best known of them, was the harmonica player Noah Lewis, who was one of the musicians who helped give Cannon's recordings their excitement a dozen years later.

The neighbors around Ripley—and around Henning, the small place a few miles closer to Memphis where Noah was born—still remember him, and they remember his music. The researcher Bengt Olsson even found members of his family. In Henning he found a cousin, Emma Green. "Noah was my cousin. He was born on Glimpse Farm in Lauderdale County, outside Henning, around 1890. His dad was Daniel Lewis. He was a farmer and didn't play no music. Noah started blowing the harp when he was nothing but a kid."

Sleepy John Estes remembers that Noah moved to Ripley with his wife when he was about seventeen. She was a cook and they lived at a small place called Minglewood. It was just outside of Ripley, a box factory at a little crossroads called Ashport. He spent most of his time playing the harmonica for whatever money he could get, and he's remembered as having a belt with harmonicas in different keys stuck in it. He'd also learned the local trick of playing two harmonicas at the same time—one with his nose—and most people remember him for this as much as anything else. Shakey Walter Horton, who lives in Chicago now but learned to play around Memphis, can still do it. Noah was a small, dark young-looking man, and his music had a deep personal sensitivity. Cannon remembers when he first met him: ". . . Noah was just a country boy from Ripley. He just played alone on parties and in the streets. Noah really could blow the harp through his nose. He had a son around Ripley by the name of Noah too who was supposed to play the harp too." When they met Cannon was thirty-three and Noah was twenty-six.

Although Noah was doing a lot of playing by himself when Cannon first went up to Ripley, there was another Ripley musician who was also playing for parties and dances with Noah, the guitarist Ashley Thompson, who's recently been found still living quietly in the country. The three of them formed a small band that played regularly around Ripley for the next three or four years, mostly on Saturday nights for country balls and suppers. Cannon, as restless as ever, went back to Memphis in 1918 and took a job as a plumber's helper, but he still kept going up to Ripley whenever there was any music to be played. But he was spending as much time on the road with the medicine shows and the small carnivals as he was playing dances in the country. By the early twenties he'd become a well-known personality for the "doctor shows," and he was on the road most of the summer, through eastern Arkansas, western Tennessee, and northern Mississippi.

The shows that Cannon traveled with were loose and informal. The "Doctor" usually had a flatbed wagon or a truck that was painted with his name and his advertising slogans, and the rest of the show straggled after the truck in their cars. They didn't travel that far—only from one small town to the next—and there wasn't much of a show to set up. The wagon worked as the stage, and if it was an afternoon show they didn't need any lights. At night they had lanterns to hang up over the show area. The show always started off with one of the singers who came out in blackface and did some blues and some jokes, or did some of the popular minstrel show songs. If there was a dancer with the show there was usually some dancing. Almost anything worked on the shows, as long as it kept people entertained. When they'd gotten enough of a crowd gathered the Doctor would come out with his product and the sales pitch would start— and it was expected to be as entertaining as the show. The Doctor promised and pleaded and harangued and argued and, sweating and shouting like a revival preacher, he dragged the money out of the crowd around the wagon. Sometimes the singers had to stay close to the audience to pass out bottles and collect money, but most of the time they went off to somebody's house, played more music, and got drunk.

Cannon toured for years, through the summer and into the big season when the cotton was coming in in late August and September and the people in the country had a little money. He was with Dr. Stokey, Dr. Benson, Dr. C.E. Hangerson, and Dr. E.B. Milton. Most of the time he played with Hosea Woods, and they had a whole repertoire of songs and jokes, but he had his own specialty number as well. It was the banjo trick he tried to do in Son Brimmer's apartment thirty years later. He'd start off playing "Old Dog Blue," then he'd suddenly swing the banjo out in front of him, over the heads of the people pressed in close to the wagon. He was still holding it by the neck, and he'd change chord as it swung back, strum it with his right hand and swing it out again. He'd finish the number with the banjo waving in front of him like a flag and the crowds usually liked it a lot. As he tried to do it later he looked down at the banjo very seriously and said that in the beginning he'd practiced for weeks to get it right, and he'd had to put a mattress down on the floor of his house so the banjo wouldn't get too damaged every time it slipped out of his hands and banged to the floor.

Hosea Woods—Cannon always called him Hosie—was about his age, from Stanton, Tennessee. They always worked out their show with a few days of rehearsals before the season started, then waited for one of the shows to get in touch with them. Hosea was a good singer and comedian and kazoo player, but he could play a little on almost every instrument. Cannon thought he was best on guitar, violin, and cornet, and they usually worked everything into the show. They did mostly old duet pieces, but Gus heard a man named Chappie Dennison playing on a piece of pipe, and he and Hosie decided to start their own jug band. At first they had a third musician who blew into a railroad coal-oil can, but Gus insists that the man blew so hard into the oil can that he kept bulging the bottom out and finally split the seams of the can. To do this a man would have to have the lung power of an air compressor, but to judge from the songs and stories coming out of that period of Southern history there would seem to have been a lot of strong men then. Whatever happened Cannon decided to play jug himself, and he had a small jug made out of sheet metal that was held in a harness that went around his neck so he could play it while he played the banjo. When he played a jug on a harness years later he usually had a kazoo stuck beside it so he could go from one to the other. The new sound gave an even more raucous noise to their songs, and Gus remembers that he would come back into Memphis at the end of the season with a new suit, in the latest box-back style, new patent-leather button shoes, and a gold watch chain hanging in front of his lapel. In a photo taken of him in Memphis about 1925 he's wearing his suit—with the belt buttoned in front—a high buttoned sweater, a dress shirt, and a fancy tie. He has the look of a cool sporting type, with none of the raffish grins of the Memphis Jug Band.

By the mid-twenties Gus had become fairly well known on the show circuit, and with one show or another he traveled from central Mississippi as far north as Virginia. He was usually called "Banjo Joe," and when the enthusiasm for country recordings finally reached the musicians in Memphis he kept the name. As Gus said years later, "I give myself the name Banjo Joe!" Son Brimmer seems to have been the person that got him interested in recording when he heard him playing on Beale Street. Gus went up to Chicago with Jim Jackson and Furry Lewis in October 1927 and auditioned for Mayo Williams at Vocalion. Williams seems to have liked his playing enough to send him over to Paramount, even though he wasn't interested in using him on his own series. Cannon remembers that when he'd auditioned for Paramount they told him they liked his playing, and they brought in Blind Blake—one of their biggest sellers and a fine guitarist—and told him to work out some pieces with Cannon. They went to Blake's apartment and spent the next three or four days rehearsing. As Cannon remembered in 1956:

We drank so much whiskey! I'm telling you we drank more whiskey than a shop! And that boy would take me out with him at night and get me so turned around I'd be lost if I left his side. He could see more with his blind eyes than I with my two good ones.

They finally got some pieces worked out and they went into the studio the first week of November. The first song was one of Cannon's blues, "Jonestown Blues," and he recorded it without Blake's guitar. Then they did three songs together, Cannon singing and playing the banjo and Blake playing his own distinctive guitar style as accompanist. The first was another blues, "Poor Boy, Long Ways from Home," then they did Cannon's wild banjo piece "Madison Street Rag," which was as much a spoken story as it was a rag, and they did an instrumental duet, "Jazz Gypsy Blues," with Cannon playing kazoo as well as banjo. Blake did one of his own songs, the widely sung minstrel show number "He's in the Jailhouse Now," and Cannon played banjo behind his singing. They finished with two of Cannon's medicine show songs, "Can You Blame the Colored Man?" and "My Money Never Runs Out." Paramount issued his songs as by "Banjo Joe with guitar accompaniment by Blind Blake," and they did some advertising for the releases. The *Chicago Defender* ran one of their mail order ads for "Madison Street Rag," with a drawing of a street scene and a photo of Cannon:

Just hear him strum that mean banjo—as the Queen looks on, and the double-jointed boy dances a jig! Here is a sensational new record by the new exclusive Paramount artist, Banjo Joe. There are some snappy words to this Blues, and a red-hot whistling solo part. In addition, Blind Blake and his Guitar do some real accompanying. All in all, it's a great record—we mean it. Be sure to ask your dealer for Paramount No. 12588, or send us the coupon.

These first Paramount recordings that Gus did are remarkable for being almost the only recordings by a black musician playing the five-string banjo, an instrument that by this time had been taken over by the white musicians who'd learned if from the black performers around them. The recordings he did for Victor were jug band music, and his banjo playing was part of the larger instru-

33

mental sound. The first song he did for Paramount, "Jonestown Blues," had only banjo accompaniment, and his playing is a virtuoso display of what can be done with the blues on a five-string instrument. It has a high, clear sound, and the strings have little resonance, so the accompaniment is much busier than a guitar accompaniment would be, but he was enough of a musician to use a wide variety of rhythms and pickings. He was nervous, and the singing sounds stiff, but he wasn't a blues singer, and the text of the song wasn't distinctive.

Said I left Lula, goin' to Jonestown
Man I left Lula, goin' to Jonestown
Those Jonestown browns, boy, make you turn your damper down.

I cried Jonestown, boy, too small a burg for me
I cried Jonestown, boy, too small a burg for me
Said I left Jonestown, boy, goin' back to Tennessee.

Say I got to old Memphis I laid my banjo down
Well I go to old Memphis I laid my banjo down
I got full of my good whiskey, my good gal made me clown.

Then I left Memphis, goin' back to Jonestown
Well, man I left Memphis, goin' back to Jonestown
Said them good old browns, boy, sure have made me clown.

It's the banjo playing that gives the record its uniqueness. He plays instrumental choruses between verses and ends with two choruses, the second in a softer picking—he introduces it by saying "Hush now, banjo"—with a kind of floating sound, like someone carrying a suitcase down a hallway as he walks on tiptoe. His banjo choruses are free, open melodies, shaped by the instrument's own distinctive sound. The banjo doesn't sustain a tone, so the slower lines of the guitar won't work on it. What Cannon has developed is a melody that uses the banjo's high brilliance, its distinctive instrumental technique using what are called "hammering-on" and "pulling-off," and the surprise of hesitations and bursts of chord. To "hammer-on" with a banjo, a string is plucked, then the left hand presses on the string with a sudden sharpness, usually a fret above the note already struck. If the finger hits the string sharply enough it will give another tone. To "pull-off," the left-hand finger lifts from the fretted string, but it lifts off with a sideways pull and plucks the string as it comes off it. He accompanies the vocal phrase with understated chording, then ends the phrase with the same melodic phrase in the banjo that he used to begin the piece. It is interesting to have Cannon's blues, if only to have this small glimpse of what the earlier banjo styles might have been as the blues was developing.

When the sessions were finished Cannon put his banjo back in its case and returned to Memphis. He and his wife had a house at 1331 S. Hyde Park, he had his job as a plumber's helper, and he had his music for the summers and falls. Chicago didn't mean that much to him. Charlie Williamson called him as soon as he was back to tell him that Victor was going to be in town to do some recordings in January, and they were looking for more jug bands. The first records by the Memphis Jug Band had been out for several months and Ralph Peer realized that he had something he could sell. As far as Cannon was concerned he'd had the first jug band in town, and he was ready to do more recording. As he said later, "There's some fellows say they started this here—I won't 'spute 'em—but I had the first jug band was heerd in Memphis." He didn't have to get the music together; he just drove up to Ripley in January and brought his old band down—Noah Lewis and Ashley Thompson. They stayed at his house, rehearsed some of their old numbers, and went into the studio the next day, a Monday, January 30, 1928. They did four songs, Ashley singing the first two, "Minglewood Blues" and "Big Railroad Blues," and Gus and Noah the two others "Madison Street Rag"—the same banjo piece he'd done with Blind Blake three months before—and "Springdale Blues." He was playing his metal jug; by this time the Victor engineers had learned how to get the sound onto the discs, and his enthusiastic puffing can be heard behind the singing.

It was a short session, but it was exciting music, and everything they played had its own distinctive character, from the sensitive "Minglewood Blues" to the rousing medicine show hokum of "Madison Street Rag." The three of them were so pleased with the session that they bought a gallon of corn whiskey and went out south of town—probably to Bunker Hill, the loose collection of run-down shacks close to the Mississippi line where a lot of the blues men hung out. They drank so much all three of them passed out, and the next morning they woke up on a cabin porch, lying on the cold, hard boards, instruments and instrument cases scattered around them, and their clothes looking as if they'd spent most of the night crawling through the dirt.

The country dance music they'd played so long flavored what they did as a jug band, and their experience gave their recordings a close, tight sound. The rhythm was built around the banjo, with its short, pungent tone, and they played in a faster 4/8 rhythm instead of the usual blues 4/4. Cannon played with a simple finger-picking, plucking one of the middle strings with his forefinger, playing the two outside strings with his thumb and second finger. It was the same kind of picking that was used by many white bands of the period, and it gives the music a heavy center to the rhythm. Cannon was looking for the rhythm in the music, and he also liked a strong bass line, stronger than he was getting from Ashley, who played a gentle, introspective finger-picking style. Peer contacted Cannon again the next summer about doing more recording, and he was out on a show with a friend, Elijah Avery, who had moved up to Memphis from Hernando, Mississippi, and was living around the corner from Cannon in Hyde Park. Elijah played a vigorous six-string banjo for the session, and Noah Lewis came down from Ripley again to play harmonica.

Their first day, September 5, 1928, they were a warm, noisy, excited country dance band—sometimes settling down into the blues, but just as often breaking out into some country ragtime or an easy shuffle. All the pieces they did were instrumentals, "Ripley Blues," "Pig Ankle Strut," "Noah's Blues," and "Hollywood Rag." Listening to them with the phonograph turned up high and a little hard liquor to drink gives you some of the feeling of what it must have been like crowded into a store or a saloon in Ripley, dancing a little, shouting to friends, the lantern hanging from the ceiling shaking with the noise and the excitement. They came back to the studio four days later, September 9, and this time they did two songs, one of them Cannon's strong, hard comment on racial differences before and after the Civil War, "Feather Bed." It was still in the forced language of the minstrel stage, but he sings it with a complete seriousness, the band hurrying behind him. Noah Lewis was playing a version of the melody "Lost John" for the chorus, and he played it with a fierceness that matched Cannon's. It was an edgy, fast, completely honest performance, and it was one of the most exciting recordings the band made. The words were hard to understand at the fast tempo they used, but enough of the bite came through, even if some of the details were lost.

I remember the time just 'fore the war,
Black man was sleepin' on shucks and straw,
Now, praise God, old massa's dead,
Black man sleepin' on a feather bed,

Ooh, ooh, my dear Henry,
Over the road I'm bound to go,
Ooh, ooh, my dear Henry,
Over the road I'm bound to go. . . .

It wasn't until later in the month, on September 20, that Hosea Woods finally got into town and had a chance to work with his old partner. He played kazoo with the others, and they did two instrumentals, "Cairo Rag" and "Bugle Call Rag." Their version of "Bugle Call Rag" is in the best medicine show tradition of doing burlesque versions of popular favorites. They traded the usual jazz breaks back and forth on kazoo and jug, with Cannon almost out of breath in all the excitement. Noah did one of the songs on the session, his beautiful "Viola Lee Blues," and there was an obscure medicine show song called "Riley's Wagon." They had done ten sides in the month, some of their best recording. Lewis was the finest harmonica player around Memphis, and his plaintive, lonely sound was a strong contrast to the brittle insistence of Cannon's banjo, and the clear, firmly outlined bass lines that Elijah Avery played. The music they did with Hosea on the last day was a suggestion of what was to come when the band got back into the McCall Building Studio the next year.

In the summer of 1929 Cannon and Hosea went out with the shows, just as they'd been doing every year; then they decided, when the season was over, to go to Chicago and see if there was anything for them there. The companies were beginning to record less, but the two of them managed to get a session with Brunswick and did two songs, "Last Chance Blues" and "Fourth and Beale" as "Cannon and Woods (The Beale Street Boys)." The session was in mid-September, and they were back in Memphis at the end of the month. Peer was in town again for Victor, and he wanted more material from the jug band. This time Cannon and Hosea stayed together, and Noah came down from Ripley again. They did four songs on October 1, "Last Chance Blues," "Tired Chicken Blues" with its interesting major-minor modality, "Goin' to Germany," and "Walk Right In," then finished their recording for the year with four more songs on October 3, "Whoa! Mule, Get Up in the Alley," "The Rooster's Crowing Blues," "Jonestown Blues," and "Pretty Mama Blues." Most of the material was from the medicine show routines that Cannon and Hosea had been doing together down in the little Mississippi towns on the hot nights at the end of harvest season. The music was noisy and exuberant, and they were so excited to be doing all of their numbers that Cannon, later, couldn't remember that Noah had come down from Ripley to record with them. He had to listen to the records, and he shook his head, finally: "I believe that boy *is* on there after all." But there were some blues, as well as the comedy songs, and Noah sang his beautiful "Goin' to Germany." The "Jonestown Blues" was the same song Cannon had done for Paramount two years before. One of the songs was to become popular later, the country ragtime duet that he and Hosea did called "Walk Right In," though at the time it was just another one of their old songs. The text was confused but it was basically about a woman telling her man to come in and sit down and think about things for a while. As Cannon explained it in *The Country Blues:*

> *I went to an old lady's house one day, and she told me, "Walk right in." I said, "I thank you." She said, "Well, will you sit down?" Said, "Thank you, ma'am." She says to me, say, "Well, how long you gonna be here?" I said, "I'll only be here but a little while." And so that night, some way or another, I commenced to dreamin'. Got up there about twelve o'clock, one night there, 1913. So I got hold of my old banjo. I said, "You know one thing, Bessie? You told me to walk in here. Now you know I'm gonna get somethin' or other on that. And this is the way it went:*

> Now you walk right in,
> Sit right down,
> Baby, let your mind roll on. . . .

By the time the records were released the stock market had crashed in the United States and the long misery of the Depression had begun. But no one knew, in the first months of it, how long it would go on, and Peer was in Memphis to record again a year later. Cannon and Hosea had come in from a show again, and, as always, Noah came down from Ripley. They did two songs on November 24, 1930, "Bring It with You When You Come," and "Wolf River

Blues," and there were two final songs on November 28, the first, ironically titled, "Money Never Runs Out" and the other "Prison Wall Blues." Hosea sang three of them—all except "Money Never Runs Out"—but he wasn't a blues singer. His voice had the high-pitched nasal tenor sound that was popular on the minstrel shows. The songs, however, were strong, musical performances, and they rounded out the series of recordings that Cannon had been doing since 1927. Cannon's Jug Stompers did twenty-six titles over its three years together—brilliant, irascible, sensitive, irrepressible, and musical. The band was all of these things, and the records have managed to catch the feeling that they had, from the sudden wailing of Noah's harmonica, to Cannon's rowdy jug playing, all of it showing their deep-rooted response to the music of the little towns and country crossroads where they did their playing.

The long years of the Depression settled over Beale Street, and what had been left of the district when the reformers cleaned it up was shut down by unemployment and poverty. There were still little jobs, street cleaning, laboring, house painting, whatever a man could find to keep going. The old wooden buildings behind Beale Street were left unpainted, and they began to have a weatherbeaten look. The larger houses back in the old neighborhoods were crowded with people living four or five to a room, and the dirt of the front yards was left untended. Fences were nailed together out of packing case boards, broken windows mended with cardboard and newspaper. The Memphis summers were still hot and drowsy, and you could go out to Bunker Hill, or back up toward Brownsville and get corn or watermelon for pennies. The bands went on working little jobs for society parties or in the country clubs. Cannon still went out with some of the old shows, though there wasn't much money when he got back in town. He was forty-seven now, he'd lived a hard, full life, and it was just as easy for him to keep his little job as a plumber's helper. Hosea still went out with him on the shows, though he sometimes worked with another friend his own age, Willie Williams.

By the forties Cannon was working as a general handyman and gardener for a white family who had a large house on South Park, one of the wealthier parts of South Memphis. There was a large garage twenty or thirty yards behind the house, and he had the apartment upstairs. The stairs went up the front of the low building, and his door was off a small balcony. He had filled every corner of the space with things he'd picked up and was going to repair or thought he might use sometime. Like all handymen he had an idea of what he could do with all of it. His banjo was in its case back by the window, next to a table piled with things he'd accumulated. He had an old picture of himself up on the wall, but he didn't have any of his old records. They'd all slipped away from him over the years. The family knew about his life as a musician, and they let him live in the apartment for a small amount of work. He spent a lot of his time working around the neighborhood cutting grass and doing general gardening. He was a familiar figure around the neighborhood, usually with a straw hat pulled down over his eyes to keep out the sun, his tools wheeled in front of him in a homemade cart. He was still the same, tall, lean, hard-muscled man he'd been for forty years and could work for hours in the long Memphis sunlight.

He was still living in the same crowded rooms when I first met him in late 1956. After the session at Son Brimmer's apartment I took him back to the house and we talked about his early years. When the record of the session came out—on Folkways in 1958—we spent a few days together and there was another chance to talk, and the people he was working for had a family party for him with the first copy of the record. Cannon sat listening to the phonograph—hearing himself talking—and he nodded his head, agreeing with everything he had to say. "That's right," he said and got out his banjo and played along with his solo. In 1959 a record was put together to go with the book *The Country Blues*, and one of the pieces on it was the old "Walk Right In." Cannon had listened to it again with the woman he'd recently married at the age of 75. "Is that my hubby on there?" she kept asking. Cannon shook his head and smiled at the song. "Me and Hosie sung that song more years than I can name. We had something in those years then."

"Walk Right In" still had some of its old excitement. In 1963 a folk group recorded a new version of it and it was suddenly a number one record, a major success. The company that had recorded it, Vanguard Records, was unsure about the copyright, and the whole problem suddenly became very complicated, with the Southern Music Corporation—Ralph Peer's company—claiming it outright. It became necessary to find Cannon, and a small group of us flew down from New York, with Maynard Solomon of Vanguard and a copyright lawyer. It took me a little time to find Cannon, since the family had left the house on South Park and Cannon and his wife had gotten their own little house on the edge of town. The son of the family knew approximately where he was, and the neighbors were watching for someone to come down. The song had been on the Memphis radio and everybody knew it was Cannon's. The house he was in was small and drafty, white painted, with two rooms. It hadn't been an easy winter for him, and he'd had to pawn his banjo. Solomon went to Beale Street, got his banjo for him, gave him money to get some coal for the house, then Cannon came to the city courthouse with us to make statements.

The interesting thing that emerged from the long, and frustrating, struggle with Cannon's copyright for the song was the glimpse it gave of Peer's method of operation in the South. Some of the singers, like Son Brimmer, had been on a royalty basis, and their songs were protected for them by Southern Music. For many other singers, however, the compositions were filed as "works for hire," which meant that the music had been written by someone working as an employee of the publishing company. With material of this kind it's always very questionable how much of it will ever earn any kind of royalty, and the companies often simply paid the performer a flat fee for the rights to the songs. Generally the writer got a larger sum this way than he would have through a royalty arrangement. Jazz musicians were notorious for selling away rights to songs for the money to pay a bar bill or a hotel account, and Fats Waller, in 1929, once signed away the rights to nine songs, including some of his biggest successes, for a few dollars each to help pay a debt. The contracts for many of Peer's artists were simply handled in the "works for hire" category. When "Walk Right In" became successful there was suddenly a great deal of money involved, and Southern's first concern was to protect their claim to the song.

Then, through the efforts of, among others, Dorothy Morrison, who had been with Southern since 1928, when the company was only Peer, herself, and a bookkeeper, an arrangement was made for Cannon to get his composer's royalties for the song, and he's gotten a small income from it over the years.

Cannon kept working through all of it, and for a time in the early sixties he had a job taking care of the lawn and the garden for a church not far from his little house. As he described it, "I got my little job cleaning up gumballs in the summer, but it don't come to much in the winter." He was one of the artists appearing in the film *The Blues*, when I was in Memphis filming in 1962, and in 1963 he was one of the three Memphis artists who came to New York for a concert with the Friends of Old-Time Music. He and Furry Lewis and Memphis Willie Borum came up in the spring on a Greyhound bus, with chicken and cake that Willie's wife had packed for them. There was an unforgettable moment when Gus first climbed the stairs of the Times Square subway one night and found himself in the middle of the lights and the hustle of 42nd Street and Broadway. He looked around shaking his head and finally said, "I never thought I'd see anything like this in all my born days." At the concert he did some of his old songs, even doing a moment of banjo juggling, and the three of them sang together as a casual jug band while Furry and Gus did their old comedy routines.

Cannon still gets around in Memphis, but he's ninety now, and even his strong arms have begun to feel a little tired. Bengt Olsson and Bill Barth, who was also doing research and playing a little music in Memphis, took Cannon up to Ripley to see Ashley Thompson, and they shook their heads a little when they saw each other, saying, "You done got old." Cannon can't play much, and he was hit in the throat when some boys tried to rob him on Beale Street, so he can't sing very well either. He is as tall and straight as ever, and in his suit jacket and horn-rimmed glasses he doesn't look as though he might have been a bluesman. But it's there in his sudden burst of laughter when he sits down, sips from a beer can, and thinks back to Ripley and Beale Street and all the other places and times he's played in his long life. "White folks, them was some times, I tell you."

4. Other Memphis Singers

Memphis wasn't a big town, and most of the musicians working along the street were with one jug band or another, but there were also some bluesmen who were brought into the studios the companies had set up in town. One of them, Jim Jackson, recorded one of the biggest blues records of the twenties, "Jim Jackson's Kansas City Blues." Jim was an older, bald singer and entertainer who was born in Hernando, Mississippi, but at the time he recorded he was living at 1150 Grant, in North Memphis. He spent most of his time with the medicine shows, and he went out with the Silas Green show, the Abbey Sutton show, also the Red Rose Minstrels, and the well-known and popular Rabbits Foot Minstrels that toured out of Port Gibson, Mississippi, every year. Most of the other Memphis musicians knew him well, played with him, and all of them knew his song "Goin' to Kansas City." Gus Cannon has said that he was in Chicago with Jim when he recorded it, but he wasn't allowed to play on the session with him. Mayo Williams had moved to Vocalion after his own blues label, Black Patti, had failed, and Jim was one of the first artists to record for him. The record was released on Vocalion 1144, Parts 1 and 2, in December 1927.

In the chaotic blues market of the late twenties it was often difficult to predict what would sell, and the companies had to put out a lot of releases to get results. Jim's song was one of those that hit. It was more of a medicine show song than a blues—a simple collection of verses like:

> If you don't want my peaches, don't shake my tree
> I ain't after that woman, but she sure likes me

followed by a refrain:

> I've got to move to Kansas City, mama, sure as you're born
> I've got to move to Kansas City, mama, sure as you're born
> I've got to move to Kansas City, honey, where they don't 'low you.

Advertisement for Jim Jackson's Kansas City Blues.

Sometimes he sang it:

I'm gonna move to Kansas City . . .

and that's the way most of the Memphis musicians remember it. The record sold and sold. On March 17, 1928, there was a full-page advertisement for it in the *Chicago Defender*, with a drawing of Jim and illustrations for all the verses. He did a second session for Vocalion—recording Parts 3 and 4 of "Jim Jackson's Kansas City Blues"—but about the same time he also began recording for Victor in Memphis. His first session for Peer was on January 30. For a brief time there was a struggle between Vocalion and Victor over his services. On April 21, 1928, only a month after the full-page ad for Vocalion, Victor announced his first two records for them, "The Policy Blues" and "Bootlegging Blues" on Vic 21268 and "My Monday Woman Blues" and "My Mobile Central Blues" on Vic 21236. The advertisement also announced that he was now an exclusive Victor artist. In May, three weeks later, Vocalion advertised its new record—"Jim Jackson's Kansas City Blues, Parts 3 and 4" on Voc 1155, but he stayed with Victor for the rest of the year, doing eighteen titles all together over the nine months he was with the company. The next year he went back to Vocalion in Chicago and did a series of recordings for them over the next year and a half.

None of Jim's records was as popular as his "Kansas City," but because it was so successful he had a chance to record an extensive repertoire of medicine show songs and blues. He'd spent his life as a country entertainer—he was probably in his late forties when he recorded—and he knew every kind of song. The thirty-one songs he recorded are a priceless glimpse of the kind of material it took to get a crowd in a country town—the kind of humor and broad slapstick that got them up to the stage and got them laughing. He wasn't a blues singer so much as he was a country songster, even though his "My Monday Woman Blues" was also sung by other Memphis blues singers. On a song like "This Mornin' She Was Gone," he could even throw in theatrical sobbing, and it only added to the loose mood of the song. He used an assumed minstrel dialect, with its conscious "gwine" and "hyar," and there were outrageous comedy songs like "I Heard the Voice of a Pork Chop," with its chorus "I heard the voice of a pork chop say, come unto me and rest."

But Jim was more than noisy country humor and tent show routines to keep the crowd listening while the next act got ready. He was a shrewdly talented man, with a deeper sense of the music he was doing. He had taken the old song "Old Dog Blue," and for years he sang it almost as a free poem, extending its imagery in the finest folk traditions. It was so startling that the one serious reviewer of the twenties, Abbe Niles, mentioned it in his column in the literary journal *Bookman* in its issue for September 1928: "Old Dog Blue . . . a wholly fascinating story of a hound who treed his possums anywhere he found them, from a holler stump to Noah's Ark." The accompaniment Jim used for it was almost a banjo picking, instead of his usual steady strum.

Had a old dog his name was Blue
You know Blue was mighty true
You know Blue was a good old dog . . .
Blue treed a possum out on a limb
Blue looked at me and I looked at him,
Grabbed that possum, put him in a sack,
Don't move, Blue, 'til I get back.
Here Ring, here Ring here,
Here Ring, here Ring here . . .

When old Blue died and I dug his grave
I dug his grave with a silver spade.
I let him down with a golden chain
And every link I called his name.
Go on Blue, you good dog you,
Go on Blue, you good dog you.
Blue lay down and died like a man
Blue lay down and died like a man
Now he's treein' possums in the promised land.

I'm going to tell you this to let you know
Old Blue's gone where good dogs go.
When I hear old Blue's bark
When I hear old Blue's bark
Blue's treed a possum in Noah's Ark
Blue's treed a possum in Noah's Ark.

There was still another dimension to Jim's skill as a performer. For a poor share cropper, in town for a Saturday's shopping, standing in a dirt street in his overalls and his sweat-stained straw hat, there would be an immediate sense of identity with something like a hound dog who finally went to heaven and treed his possums with the angels. In many of the songs that he did there was an even more direct identification of the subject of the song with the determined sense of life in his audience. The blues had to function as the language of a culture that was almost deprived of a language, and in it there was a whole range of expression that went beyond the simple response to loneliness or poverty. To a white who happened to come along and stand back of the crowd to listen to someone like Jim Jackson, it would sound like the usual "darkey" songs he'd heard all his life. Stealing chickens, getting in trouble with the police, getting run out of town—all the clichés of the minstrel shows. And the singers were usually wearing blackface with white-painted mouths, so there wasn't much to make him think any differently. But Jim was saying more; he was saying that the black man will keep on going, he won't be beaten, that he'll somehow get through it.

Jim's songs weren't the only ones that had this deeper intention—there are well-known examples like "The Gray Goose," who couldn't be cut or eaten, or "Long John Green from Bowling Green," who couldn't be caught. But he was able to do it in the guise of something else, and the most obvious comic song could become a sudden sharp comment on something that was much larger. He did a version of the "traveling man" song and he presented it as a simple minstrel song. The man made his living "stealin' chickens," which immediately established his color, since in the popular songs of the period the black man's life was spent stealing chickens. The policeman went after him, but

> He didn't care how fast that a freight train would pass
> This man would get on board.

Jim went on singing in a cheerful voice, with a simple strum on the guitar, for the next verse reciting a well-known "brag" story about the man.

> Well, they sent that old travelin' man one day,
> I asked for one pail of water,
> And where he had to go was two miles and a quarter.
> He went and got that water alright, but he stumbled and fell down.
> He run three miles and a half and got another pitcher,
> Caught the water 'fore it hit the ground.

His last verse was more specific, and on the words "white ladies" he sang with a little mincing lilt, to make it even sharper, to make it even more clear that in the contest between the two the black man was going to come through.

> He ran and jumped on this Titanic ship
> And started up that ocean blue.
> He looked out and spied that big iceberg, and right overboard he flew.
> All the white ladies on the deck of the ship
> Said that man certainly was a fool,
> But when that Titanic ship went down he's shootin' craps in Liverpool.

> Don't you know,
> He was a traveling man. . . .

He repeated the last two lines, as a kind of insistent reminder.

> And he wouldn't give up and he wouldn't give up
> 'Til the police shot him down.
> And he wouldn't give up and he wouldn't give up
> 'Til the police shot him down.

Though he had veiled it in the most obvious minstrel show terms, his audience, in the small Mississippi towns where he did most of his playing, had no difficulty understanding what he was saying.

For Jim, as for almost everyone else, the bleak first months of the Depression finished the recording sessions. In the early winter of 1930, probably February, Vocalion was in Memphis to record and he did two songs, "Hesitation Blues (Oh! Baby, Must I Hesitate?)" and "St. Louis Blues," that were released later in the year on Vocalion 1477. The local musicians don't remember seeing him after this—they don't remember that he was in town much after the success of his first record. Sometime in the thirties he seems to have gone back to Hernando, and he died there in 1937.

Another singer that the musicians knew from the tent shows and from Beale Street was a tall, heavy man named Jack Kelly. Furry Lewis remembers him living in Orange Mound, but Willie Borum, who played with him a lot in the thirties, remembers him living in town. "Jack Kelly smoked a cigar all the time. It was never lit, it just always was there. . . . He would play the guitar and I would blow the harp. Doc Higgs was with us on jug." Although he worked along the street, he had a steady group that was managed by Howard Yancey. Will Batts played violin and was as much of a leader as the band had. Sometimes Stokes and Dan Sane played with them, sometimes a banjo player named Ernest Motley, and later the guitarist Milton Robie. Mary Batts, Will's widow, remembers that they rehearsed at their house all the time and that most of their jobs were for Memphis white people, who brought them out to picnics or the country club and then relied on Jim Strainer to drive them back when they got drunk. She would tell him just to "Bring him up there on the porch," and she'd let Will sleep there until he was sober enough to come in the house. Will had played violin on Frank Stokes's last session for Victor, and though he had a day job all through the years, he went out and played along Beale Street with the rest of them when he got through with work.

As the thirties ground on there was an effort to revive the record industry, and the labels manufactured by the American Recording Corporation continued to release blues material. Kelly, with the band, got a session in New York on August 1, 2, and 3, 1933. Dan Sane made the trip, with Will Batts and "Doctor" D.M. Higgs, who was playing the jug. Mary Batts remembers that Will played the guitar with Jack on the first song, "Highway No. 61 Blues," and after Jack had sung five numbers Will sang two. The next day Dan did the first song, as in the Memphis Jug Band days when everybody got to try a blues. Even Doc Higgs sang a "Bad Luck Blues," but the titles he and Dan sang on were never released. The singing on the third day was by Jack and Will. Will was a slight, dark, good-looking man who had been playing and singing in Memphis for most of his life. He was born on January 24, 1904, in Benton County, west of Michigan City, Mississippi, but he moved to Memphis with his family when he was fifteen. His father played the violin, as well as his older brother Robert, and Will started playing at country suppers when he was nine. They had to put him up on a chair so people could see him.

There was still enough interest in the jug band sound for ARC to call them a jug band—"Jack Kelly and his South Memphis Jug Band"—but what they played was mostly solid, strong blues with a heavy accompaniment. They did one instrumental that was released, "Policy Rag," but the rest of the songs were blues. Kelly was a deep-voiced singer, with a kind of stolid feel for his music. There wasn't any of the kind of instrumental arranging that Son Brimmer had tried with the Memphis Jug Band. They recorded blues with a thick texture and an insistent rhythm, loping along after Doc Higgs's jug playing. The records were released on the ARC low-price labels.

Jack recorded again in Memphis in the late thirties—for Vocalion on July 14, 1939. He did ten sides, and six of the songs were finally released. There was another guitar and a violin with him, but no jug. The band never made much money from their recording, but Mary Batts remembers that Will came back from the first New York trip with " . . . a whole fruit jar full of money!" The Swedish researcher who talked to Mrs. Batts, Bengt Olsson, has also suggested that Jack recorded again in 1950 with the harmonica player Walter Horton, who was living in Memphis during this period—before he went to Chicago to join the Muddy Waters band. A Sun release, Sun 174, is listed on the label as by "Jackie Boy and Little Walter," and one of the composers credited is Kelly. Horton insists that they recorded together, so the Sun record probably is the one he remembers. Only the label has been found, but a copy, if it ever turns up, should make it clear whether or not it is Jack Kelly. Willie Borum remembers that Jack was an old man, gray-haired, when he died. Will Batts had died earlier, of a stroke in 1956, and Mary gave Jack Will's guitar. Jack died in Memphis, probably around 1960.

Son and the Memphis Jug Band used nearly every musician in town for their sessions, but Vocalion was interested in getting something for themselves out of it, and on their last Memphis session—the same trip when they recorded Jim Jackson's last songs—they recorded a tent show entertainer named Jed Davenport and his Beale Street Jug Band. Not much is known about Davenport except that he was working the shows with Dub Jenkins on saxophone and Al Jackson on bass. He'd recorded two harmonica solos the fall before for Vocalion and they might have suggested that he come in with a jug band on their next trip. They did six sides in January 1930, with two different harmonica players, two guitars, and a jug. The songs were loose and uninhibited. Someone played mandolin on one of the songs; there was a kazoo on "Piccolo Blues" but it's impossible to tell who could be playing. They probably played with Memphis Minnie on a session the next summer, in August, but there were only two titles—"Grandpa and Grandma Blues" and "Garage Fire Blues"—and the band was called Memphis Minnie and Her Jug Band. Davenport was said to have picked up the trumpet and by the late thirties he was working in local clubs. He left Memphis for a time—it's been suggested he was drafted during the Second World War—but was back along Beale Street in the 1960s.

At the same time, however, another Memphis bluesman was creating music that came from other sources and tied itself more closely to older song tradition. Furry Lewis had been part of the jug band crowd. His own music was distinct and individual, adding his own mood and style to the music in Memphis.

5.
Furry Lewis

Furry Lewis is a small, gentle man who spent most of his life sweeping the streets of Memphis. If you saw him working along Beale Street, or Hernando, or Vance—the streets he swept for more than forty years—you wouldn't have thought of him as a bluesman. He pushed a can in front of him on a wheeled metal cart, sweeping as he went, leaving full cans at the street corners for the city trucks to pick up, and taking empties where they'd been left for him. In the summers he usually wore a short-sleeved shirt, wash trousers, and a base-ball cap. He limped a little; he lost a leg in a railroad accident in 1917 and he swept Memphis streets for more than forty years on an artificial leg. It was a morning job, and he started out before there was much traffic, always seeing the same few regulars along the streets, people who, like him, had something to get ready for a new day. He was usually through by eleven or twelve. In the summers he worked as much as he could in the shade, to get away from the sun, and in the winters he stopped off a lot in buildings where he knew somebody who'd let him sit for a moment to warm up.

He moved around a lot during those years, and if you came into town and had to find him you went down to the city garage, where the sanitation crews were dispatched. Once you tracked down the crew boss in the empty, echoing build-ing, he would look at his chart and tell you where Furry was. "He's got Beale Street to do again—let's see, it's about 9:30, he should be right about here now"— and he'd show you a point on his city map, and off you'd go looking for Furry. When you found him, usually not far from where the crew boss said he'd be, he kept working as he talked. He just worked a little slower and stayed close to the curb so he could hear what you were saying. It wasn't much of a job, but it kept him going through all the lean years, and he finally had a small pension out of it at the end.

When Furry went to work for the Sanitation Department in 1923, his other life, in a way, was over, and after he'd worked many years there his other life was almost lost in the shadowy days people thought of when they reminisced about Beale Street. When you'd find him in whatever furnished room he was living in and you'd bring over a guitar and something to drink so he could play again, most of the people living in the house with him would hang around the door looking at him with surprise. They'd never known he was anything but a street sweeper. If they had heard anything about his old life they hadn't really believed it. But there had been the other life, and for a few scattered days in the late twenties, he took time off from his job and took his guitar to the studios set up in Chicago or Memphis, first recording for Vocalion, then for Victor. There weren't many sessions—four of them—and there weren't many recordings—only twenty songs—but they were enough to give Furry a secure place in the history of blues.

The songs Furry sang were distinctly personal, while still, in many way, characteristic of the blues in Memphis. He's almost an archetypal figure in the development of the blues in the city, even though it was the street bands, rather than solo blues artists, who were the most obvious along Beale Street. Even Furry, when he remembers the old days, usually remembers playing on Beale Street with a group. As he said in a conversation with Bengt Olsson years later:

> *When I was eighteen, nineteen years old, I was good. And when I was twenty I had my own band and we could all play. Had a boy named Ham, played jug. Willie Polk played the fiddle and another boy, call him Shoefus, played the guitar, like I did. All of us North Memphis boys. We'd meet at my house and walk down Brinkley to Poplar and go up Poplar to Dunlap or maybe all the way down to Main. People would stop us on the street and say, "Do you know so-and-so?" And we'd play it and they'd give us a little something. Sometimes we'd pick up fifteen or twenty dollars before we got to Beale. . . .*

The blues in Memphis didn't have the intense, raw loneliness of Mississippi music. It was a softer, talkier blues—mingled with the medicine show songs and folk songs and ballads that were popular in the country when the musicians left town to play the little shows. The other Memphis bluesmen who did a fair amount of recording—Jim Jackson and Frank Stokes—like Furry mixed minstrel songs with their blues, and their ragtime songs were as popular as anything else they did. All of them were from Mississippi, and they heard the blues there, but Memphis was different, and its music was different. Furry had been born in Mississippi—his name is Walter, and he's still not sure why other children at school gave him the name Furry—but he left it when he was still a boy, and his life has been spent in Memphis, most of it in the run-down neighborhood of old wood-sided houses lining narrow, badly paved streets north of the business section. He thought for many years that he was born in 1900, and he stayed on his job until he thought he'd gotten to retirement age. But one of the young blues enthusiasts who was taking guitar lessons from Furry, Jerry Finberg, went through old school records to help Furry get Medicaid and found that he'd been born seven years earlier, on March 6, 1893. Occasionally Furry himself will forget and give other dates, but this seems to be the correct one. When he finally stopped sweeping the streets he was in his seventies. He was born south of Jackson, in Greenwood, Mississippi, but he, his mother, and his two sisters moved to Memphis when he was six. She'd separated from his father before he was born, and Furry never saw him. His life was spent in Memphis, with occasional small trips out of the city. As he told Bengt Olsson:

My mother had a sister lived on Brinkley Avenue. Call it Decatur now. We stayed with her. They a housing project there now, but I could still show you the spot. I was raised right there and walked a few block to the Carnes Avenue School. Went to the fifth, and that's as far as I got. Started going about, place to place, catching the freights. That's how I lost my leg. Goin' go down a grade outside Du Quoin, Illinois. I caught my foot in a coupling. They took me to a hospital in Carbondale. I could look right out my window and see the ice-cream factory. That was in 1916. I had two or three hundred dollars in my pocket when that happened, too. I had just caught a freight 'cause I didn't feel like spending the money for a ticket.

It was Furry's Memphis background that helped shape his blues, that gave him the kind of straightforward singing style, without embellishment or stress, that was characteristic of most of the blues records the Memphis men made. The same quiet, almost thoughtful understatement was part of everything they did, from blues to minstrel show songs, to folk ballads. They sang all kinds of material for the little shows, and Furry will probably always be remembered best not for his blues but for his brilliant reworking of the great ballads "Casey Jones," "John Henry," and "Stackerlee." But his first two sessions were blues, done for Jack Kapp, who was director of the Vocalion race series that Mayo Williams was auditioning talent for. Furry remembers that he had been out with a show singing with Jim Jackson, and Vocalion brought them up to Chicago because Jim's song "Goin' to Kansas City" was very popular locally. Furry feels they went up in May together, then they were auditioned separately; but Jim didn't record his "Jim Jackson's Kansas City Blues" until a fall session, when Furry did his second group of blues for Vocalion, so he probably has confused the two trips. He does, however, remember the first afternoon he was in the studio and described it when we first talked in 1959:

The first recording session, when I was around, goin' around then, you know, gettin' people could play, and we was goin' to Chicago, you know, to make records. And so I went on there and I met Mr. Jack Kapp. He's a fine fellow, Mr. Jack Kapp was a fine fellow, and so I made two or three records there with Mr. Jack Kapp. When I first went in there, you know, he know'd what I like and so he had a whole gallon of whiskey sittin' there and he said, "Well, you drink a little, but just don't drink too much until you get through with the record because you get so drunk you can't play." So, I like to got drunk anyway, but I made the record. . . .

51

Furry did five blues his first session, "Rock Island Blues," "Everybody's Blues," "Jelly Roll," "Mr. Furry's Blues," and "Sweet Papa Moan." They seem to have been well enough received for Vocalion to bring him back again with Jim Jackson in the fall, and all of the releases were advertised in the *Chicago Defender*; so Furry, in a quiet way, had begun his recording career. Jim Jackson did his "Kansas City Blues" at his session, and it became one of the biggest blues hits of the twenties. Furry, at the same time, was recording another group of blues, but he began the session with the first of his great ballad versions, "Stackerlee," which was titled "Billy Lyons and Stock O'Lee." This time the blues didn't do well enough for Vocalion to bring him up the next spring, but Ralph Peer was in Memphis the next summer—recording, among other people, Jim Jackson, who had moved from Vocalion—and he did a session with Furry. On August 28, a Tuesday, Furry took the afternoon off from his job, changed his clothes, and went down to their studio in the McCall Building. It was a long session, and he did seven blues and a magnificent reworking of the ballad "Casey Jones" that was released on both sides of Vic 21664 with the new title "Kassie Jones"—probably so Peer could published the version with his own publishing house.

The blues he did for Peer were also interesting, among them the brilliantly accompanied "I Will Turn Your Money Green" and his "Dry Land Blues," but they don't seem to have sold well since Peer didn't use him again. But Vocalion was in Memphis again the next fall—in 1929—and Furry did his last session in the twenties. The first two sides were another ballad—this time his "John Henry," released on Voc 1474 as "John Henry (The Steel Driving Man)"—and he finished with two more blues, "Black Gypsy Blues" and "Creeper's Blues." Furry's first recording career, and to a large extent his creative years as a bluesman were over with these sessions; he never was able again to create songs with the vividness and the uniqueness of the finest recordings he did then.

All of the blues that Furry did were interesting, and everything was a skillful example of setting an accompaniment to a melody, but the three ballads were especially his own. For "Billy Lyons and Stock O'Lee" he used a repeated line that seemed to sum up the song: "When you lose your money learn to lose." As he explains it, "That means don't be no *hard* loser. That's what this song is about." That *is* what "Stackerlee" is about, but few singers have been interested in any dimension to the song beyond Stackerlee and the murder of his friend Billy Lyons. It is this sudden, quiet summing up of a song that makes his ballads stay in the memory. He's been able to find the essence of the songs, the feeling of quiet melancholy that threads through them, tying the details of the story into a broader, deeper, more human narrative. The gentle sadness is part of the wistful, almost tentative quality of his singing, and he emphasized it with the guitar accompaniments. The finger-picking he used for "Kassie Jones," with a slide on the lower strings, suggest some of the feeling of the train and even has the quality of a second melody of its own—sad, in its way, and lonely.

In both "Kassie Jones" and "John Henry" he changed the emphasis of the songs by focusing on the women and the other people around the central figures. In the usual versions of "Casey Jones" he's presented as a brave but reckless engineer who tries to make up for lost time, wrecks the trains, and dies ". . . with his hand on the throttle," scalded with steam. Furry, instead, talks about Casey's wife and a dream she had that she never explains. "Mrs. Casey says she dreamt a dream, the night she bought her sewing machine . . . " He talks about Casey and his troubles with the police almost as though he were reminiscing about the times he ran into Casey himself—in barrooms or on the street—or as though he were simply repeating things someone else had told him. He repeats the last line of each verse almost thoughtfully—and the lines still linger while he plays the sad little guitar melody before the next verse. "This mornin' I heard someone was dyin', Mrs. Casey's children on the doorstep cryin'." The mood isn't broken, even when Casey's widow tells the children not to worry, there will be more pension money for them. Instead, you hear over and over again the same little refrain, the same mood of quiet reminiscence. Furry has humanized, personalized the long story of Casey Jones—taking away the trappings of heroism and the religious clichés that were standard in the versions he heard around him.

His "John Henry" had the same quality, and he again stripped the ballad of its heroic overtones. He makes it clear that it was a human being who dies—and left sad people behind him. There were women in other versions of "John Henry," and he includes them all, but there is a poignant sadness in the image of John Henry's woman going to find him. "I'm going where John Henry fell dead. Please take me where my man fell dead." Like John Hurt, who recorded his version of the ballad as "Spike Driver's Blues," Furry finds the story more tragic than heroic. As in "Kassie Jones," he repeats the last line of each verse, emphasizing the mood, and again the accompaniment follows what he's doing with his voice and in the text. The accompaniment is done with a slide, in the Mississippi bottleneck style, and the guitar states the melody in a lingering minor version of it while the thumb, alternating on the first and third lower strings of the guitar, relentlessly drives the rhythm. He still plays it the same way, and his fingers seem to dance on the strings. Watching him play it is almost like watching a ballet done with his hands, as Chaplin had done his ballet with two buns on forks.

The imagery of Furry's blues, in his first sessions, was a hard contrast to the soft melancholy of his ballads. The images in song after song were rough and cruel, the relationships with women described in angry recitals of infidelity and disappointment. In one blues he sang:

> I believe I'll buy me a graveyard of my own,
> Believe I'll buy me a graveyard of my own.
> I'm goin' kill eve'body that have done me wrong. . . .

Even though this verse, as well as almost every other verse he used, came from earlier blues sources, he seems to insist on saying this over and over again. His relationships with women seem to have been as disappointing for him.

> I'd rather see my coffin rollin' from my door,
> Rather see my coffin rollin' from my door,
> Than to hear my good girl says I don't want you no more. . . .

Again, from another blues:

> I'd rather hear the screws on my coffin sound,
> I'd rather hear the screws on my coffin sound,
> Than to hear my good girl says I'm jumpin' down. . . .

He could say with sudden bitterness:

> If you want to go to Nashville, mens, ain't got no fare,
> Want to go to Nashville, mens, ain't got no fare.
> Cut your good girl's throat and the judge will send you there. . . .

> I'm goin' get my pistol, forty rounds of ball,
> Get my pistol, forty rounds of ball.
> I'm goin' shoot my woman just to see her fall.

Verses like these, of course, were standard material for many blues of the period, but it was Furry's insistence on them that gives them an emotional weight. Often his songs, like "Falling Down Blues," were simply loose collections of verses, and most of the verses he used were part of the standard Memphis repertoire, but he could put them together with a close sensitivity to the verse's inner meaning. He didn't do it with any kind of intellectual preconception. When I asked him about it as part of the research for the book *The Poetry of the Blues* in the summer of 1962 he said:

> *Well, one thing, when you write the blues and what you be thinkin' about, you be blue, and you ain't got nothin' hardly to think about you just already blue and jus' goin' write.*

In answer to a question as to how he put the verses together he said:

> *Well, you just rhyme 'em up. See, the time when you just get a blues, what you call the blues sometimes you just haven't come out like you 'sposed to and it don't be right you have to go all over again until you rhyme it. It got to be rhymed just like it is 'cause if you call yourself with the blues or anything else, if it ain't rhymed up it don't sound good to me or nobody else, do it.*

He didn't feel there was any principle of structuring in the way he developed his texts. Asked about his choice of a first verse he said:

Well, the way that'll be, the first verse is just—the first verse could be the last. You know, just any old verse I wanted that could have that to the first, then go right on from there and just rhyme up from it, and make them all kind of match, you know, the same like that.

His only general consideration was that every verse should be ". . . talking about the same thing." But he interpreted this very loosely, and each of his songs contained verses that seemed to have been chosen almost by accident. But often it's possible to sense a sequence even in a blues that seems to have little inner connection. In one of his songs he moves from a verse dealing with a "graveyard of my own," to the cynical verse about killing a woman to get to Nashville; then he uses a verse about shooting his own woman—which brings it a step closer to him, since the second verse was a general reference to "mens." He follows this in the next verse by saying that he'd rather hear the screws on his coffin than hear that his woman is "jumpin' down"—leaving him. These first four verses have been related by their general mood of anger at his woman's leaving him. The next three verses seem to bring it even closer to him. He says that he's going to sit down and write a letter, ". . . back to yon' town." Then:

This ain't my home, I ain't got no right to stay.
This ain't my home, must be my stoppin' place.

The reason for the letter becomes clear—he's left home and he's writing back. The song ends:

When I left my home you would not let me be,
When I left my home you would not let me be.
Wouldn't rest contented 'til I come to Tennessee.

With this he seems to clarify the entire text. He's angry and bitter as the song begins—angry because his woman is leaving him. And her leaving him is even harder because she forced him to leave home—to "come to Tennessee"—and she's left him alone there. In another place, and another time—perhaps even a few minutes later—Furry might have sung it differently and used different verses in a different order, but what he sang here seems to have been conceived with some inner coherence in mind, even if it wasn't consciously articulated.

As a guitarist Furry had few peers in Memphis in the twenties and he seemed to have learned every kind of picking and tuning in his wanderings into the countryside. "Falling Down Blues" was played with a slide, with the same alternating thumb bass he used for "John Henry," barring across the frets with a finger to make the change to a subdominant harmony. His "Mean Old Bedbug"—a cover version of Lonnie Johnson's big success—was finger-picked with a kind of banjo style that used a pull-off with the left hand to give it a little halting rhythm. "Why Don't You Come Home"—his version of the Memphis song "Goin' to Brownsville"—was played with a bottleneck, the guitar respondins to the vocal line in a beautiful interrelationship between the voice and the sliding "song" on the guitar that followed it. Of all his pickings probably the most interesting was the complex accompaniment he used for "I Will Turn Your Money Green," the second song he recorded for Ralph Peer on August 28, 1928. The text was one of his less coherent assemblies, with the second verse, the well-known "If you follow me, baby, I will turn your money green . . ." used almost arbitrarily for the title. But the picking was distinctive and inventive. The guitar was tuned to open D, which is D-A-D'-F#-A'-D''—and the rhythm was a strong counterpoint to the simple melody.

In most of the blues he sang in the twenties, he'd been harsh and angry about the women he'd known, but there were other verses, other glimmerings of relationships that had been happier, of love that hadn't ended with such bitterness. It was one of the women who'd known him and been happy with him then who led me to the small room where he was living in Memphis in 1958. It was winter, and it was cold along Beale Street, and I didn't have any recording to do, but I still took the chance to stop by and talk to Will Shade again in the shabby room where he was living with Jenny Mae. After an hour or so of talking about the city's bluesmen, Will went out of the room to get his guitar and Jenny Mae came close to the old iron stove against the wall. "Those other men you asked about," she said in a quiet voice, "Furry Lewis doesn't live too far from here. I saw him on the corner yesterday. He's working for the city." She and Furry had lived together before she was with Will and they still talked whenever she saw him on the street.

The city garage was empty when I stopped in later in the afternoon—all the crews had gone home for the day—but the office suggested calling the Memphis city personnel office. After two or three phone calls a girl said she had an address that she thought was current. Late the same afternoon I found Furry sitting in his room in the house the girl had given me the address for, a frame house on one of the North Memphis back streets. The street was lined with other houses like it, a few straggling trees, automobiles along the curb, straggling bits of lawn, the houses shabby and unpainted—here and there one of the older ones torn down and a new brick apartment unit up in its place. He was surprised that someone had finally come to talk to him again, but he was easy about it, too. It had been a long time of sitting in rented rooms and getting up before dawn to go out and sweep the streets. The next day I had an old Epiphone guitar I'd rented from one of the Beale Street pawnshops when he got back to his room from the job. He took the guitar, checked the tuning, and asked me what I wanted to hear. I was surprised that he didn't want to try the guitar first, but I asked, after a moment of uncertainty, for "John Henry" the way he'd played it thirty years before. It didn't have all of his old presence or sense of drama, but his fingers were almost as fast as ever, and his voice still had its gentle, soft plaintiveness.

Furry and I were able to do a considerable amount of recording over the next two years. A few songs were recorded in February 1959—then the rest of an LP for Folkways was completed in his room in October. He had told his neighbors in advance and the recording was done with the door of the room left open so people could stand inside and listen. He was pleased and excited to be recording again—as much for the chance to show everyone that he was one of the old Beale Street bluesmen as for the money or the chance to be on record. Two years later, in the spring of 1961, Ken Goldstein, who was in charge of the Prestige Bluesville series, asked for two more albums. There was time to write Furry in advance, and when I got to Memphis he had a guitar ready and a carefully lettered list of songs. As he got into the car to go to the studio he stopped and waved the guitar to everyone from the neighborhood who'd come out on their porches to watch. "Goin' to do some recordin'," he said several times, then got into the car with a pleased smile.

The Prestige sessions were held in Sun Studios, the modern recording facilities that Sam Phillips had built after his success with Sun Records and his group of artists that included Elvis Presley, Jerry Lee Lewis, Carl Perkins, and Johnny Cash. The engineer for the sessions was Scotty Moore, who had been the guitar player on all of Elvis's first recordings and was still working with Elvis whenever he was doing a film. If Furry felt any nervouness at the empty studio and the elaborate control room he never showed it. His only worry was whether or not he had enough songs to fill two LPs. He'd been working on the guitar, and he could do all of his old pickings except the accompaniment to "Turn Your Money Green." He still sang many of his old blues, but they had become gentler, and there wasn't so much anger in the verses he used.

The sessions went slowly, but it wasn't Furry's fault. Scotty was as much a musician as he was an engineer, and at almost every song they stopped so Scotty could ask him what tuning he was using, and how he was picking the accompaniment. Unlike so many white guitarists who have come to Furry with the same questions, Scotty wasn't trying to learn something he could use himself. It was just his quiet appreciation of what Furry was doing as an artist and a musician. Furry used every kind of tuning, usually working with open tunings so he could get the sound of the open string vibration. This is a fuller sound than a fretted string, and the fullness of his open tunings added to the depth of his guitar sound. Also he kept the guitar tuned low, sometimes almost a fourth below concert pitch, again for the fuller resonance he got with the slacker strings. He was able to take one day off work, but the second afternoon he had to come after he'd finished sweeping the streets. There was more money for him after the sessions, but it was still the chance to be a musician again that meant the most to him.

In 1962 the film *The Blues* was conceived, mostly because of Furry and the flashing pattern of his fingers as he picked "John Henry." It seemed that film was the only way to capture what he was doing. In July it was possible to film him working out on his job—sweeping along one of the sidewalks not far from Beale. Then he did his "John Henry" in front of his house with his new wife, Versie, and his friends, in their best clothes, listening to him play. He had a small, old guitar that he'd decorated with a ribbon on the neck and the ribbon and the movement of his fingers created the same kind of free dance that I'd first seen three years before. It was still difficult to find a way for him to get out and play more, but the new recordings were selling a little, and in the early sixties there was a growing interest in the country blues.

In the spring of 1963 Furry, along with Gus Cannon and Memphis Willie Borum, rode a Greyhound up from Memphis to play a concert in New York City sponsored by the Friends of Old Time Music. It was intended more as a jug band concert than a blues concert, so they played as a group for most of the evening—for an audience of about two hundred that had gathered in one of the small lecture halls at New York University. But there was a completely unplanned and unforgettable moment in the Village Folklore Center on MacDougal Street in Greenwich Village earlier in the day. All three of them had come into the shop, and they were standing toward the back talking with Israel Young, the owner. A boy came in with his girl, both of them in their teens, and he picked up one of the shop's guitars. He told her he was going to play a Furry Lewis picking for her—completely unaware that Furry was also in the shop. As he played Furry came closer to him, listening, and as the boy looked up and hesitated, Furry reached out without a word, took the guitar, and showed how the lick *really* should be played. He finished with a medicine show buck and wing, tapped twice on the body of the guitar, handed it back, and with a half smile pushed his hat down on his forehead and walked back to Gus and Willie, leaving the boy with the guitar and a very confused expression on his face.

In the years since then Furry has finally retired from his job and taken his small pension. He moved from room to room for a while, as he and Versie quarreled and separated and made up and came back together. As the blues revival became more widespread he began to travel more and there was some more recording. He's become part of the small folk and blues music scene in Memphis, appearing at the Memphis Blues Festival, and working for occasional club jobs. He hasn't changed, and he's still the same gentle, small man he was, though he remembers more of his old medicine show jokes now, so there's more laughter in his room. His fingers have finally gotten slower, but his voice still has it quiet plantiveness. He had never completely stopped playing, thinking that sometime, somehow, the music might come back. It has now, in ways he never thought it would, and it brought him a new life and vitality, at a moment when he thought his life was almost over. As he told an interviewer who talked with him later,

> . . . All those years I kept working for the city, thinking things might change, Beale Street might go back like it was. But it never did. . . . Sometimes, nothing to do, no place to play, I'd hock the guitar and get me something to drink. And then I'd wish I had it, so I could play, even just for myself. I never quit playing, but I didn't play out enough for people to know who I was. Sometimes I'd see a man, a beggar, you know, playing guitar on the sidewalk, and I'd drop something in his cup, and he wouldn't even know who I was. He'd think I was just a street sweeper.

6.
Frank Stokes

Now listen baby, you so good and sweet,
Hey, little baby, you so good and sweet,
I want to stay 'round you, if I have to beg in the street.

For many of the bluesmen of the twenties there's no way to tell what they looked like—only occasional handbills and leaflets, a badly reproduced photo of a face in a faded old record catalog—a guitar, a stiff expression, and an uncomfortable suit. Paramount Records used a photo of Frank Stokes and Dan Sane—"The Beale Street Sheiks"—on an advertising leaflet in 1928, in their suits, holding their guitars. But even though their faces were hard to see, there was still a sense of their presence, their strength, despite the stiff pose and the uncomfortable clothes.

You just can't help it, the way the Beale Street Sheiks play their big time numbers on Paramount Records tempts you to get every one of them. They have some new records waiting, ready to give you more than your money's worth.

But there's still another photo of Frank Stokes—from the Victor catalog the next year—and this seems to be more the way he's remembered by the people who knew him in Memphis. He's in his shirt sleeves, with light-colored suspenders, a cloth cap pulled down over his forehead, and the inevitable guitar in his hands, but it's held out there in front of him as if he really were going to play it. His face is dark, with a thin moustache, intent eyes, and a strong, set mouth. Will Batts was the violinist on Frank's last sessions for Victor, and Will's sister, Maggie Tuggle, still remembered Frank when being interviewed by Bengt Olsson.

Frank Stokes? He was very tall. He used to play for picnics. Once I was giving a party and Frank Stokes was playing there. Just when he began playing everyone began dancing. There was a fat woman who stomped, so that a floor-seal popped! Stokes played with a beat that was very good for dancing. Him and Will used to play "Sweet Georgia Brown." Will played the violin. I loved to hear them play that.

Despite the differences between them in age and temperament the Memphis musicians were a group. They lived and played and hustled together. Every bluesman from the twenties remembered Frank, and they all describe him as a tall, strong man, older than they were, who had a blacksmith shop and did most of his playing with Dan Sane (or Sain), a close friend who was with him until the late forties when Sane moved to Caruthersville, Missouri. Stokes lived south of the city—southeast, toward the Mississippi line—and his blacksmith shop was in Oakville, on the corner of Democrat Lane. There are different opinions about his age. Some of the people who knew him said he would have been over sixty when he had his picture taken for Paramount. Willie Borum, who played with both Frank and his son in the thirties, thought that Frank would have been in his fifties. Part of the confusion is that he didn't come into town until the twenties and he went back to Mississippi before his death. Mary Batts, Will Batts's widow, knew him very well and she thought he must have been born about 1880, which would make him in his late forties when he was recording. The people who were close to him knew him as a musician, and his age wasn't important.

It wasn't only their loose association playing on Beale Street that bound the musicians together. They were just as much joined by their Mississippi background. An old friend, Lizzie Wise, said that Frank came from Tutwiler, south of Clarksdale, where he was raised by a Fred Carbin. From Tutwiler he moved to Hernando, Mississippi, a kind of center for drifting singers and guitar players, where he played with Jim Jackson, Elijah Avery, and younger bluesmen like Robert Wilkins and Garfield Akers. People still remember him working for the Doctor Watts Medicine Show with Akers—both of them with their faces blacked up, except for the usual painted white mouth. Dan Sane, who was to work with him later, was also from Hernando, and their association probably began there. Hernando isn't far from Memphis—just a few miles below the state line—and most of the musicians found their way into the city at one time or another in their careers. Fred Carbin moved into Memphis, and Stokes, who was still living with him, came in as well, and they had a house in Bunker Hill.

Bunker Hill is still a section of wooden houses with tumbledown fences straggling along the pitted roads. Stokes always was a traveling man, and he was gone a lot—two months a year back in Olive Branch, Mississippi, and down into the Delta for picking season—but Bunker Hill was what he thought of as home, and he had a wife there named Lula. She still is living, and she remembers that they moved together when he went to Oakville and started the blacksmith shop there. She said that he played every Saturday night in Oakville—outside the J.J. Arnold Grocery Store. "If you was there on Sat'day night you just couldn't get through in no way. The place was crowded as could be . . . white folks too; they was crazy 'bout Frank—called him lots of times 'cause they wanted him to play for 'em. Played all those foxtrots and waltzes for 'em.''

Frank also sang a blues about Bunker Hill, where they first lived, but Bunker Hill was well known to Memphis bluesmen, and there was an even earlier recording of a song about it by Ollie Rupert, who sang in 1927:

Out on Bunker Hill, where the people have their fun,
Out on Bunker Hill, where the people have their fun,
I can lay down on the green grass and look up at the sun.

Frank did play all those "foxtrots and waltzes," and he also sang medicine show songs as well as blues—old street pieces like "Chicken You Can Roost behind the Moon" and "Mister Crump Don't Like It," known and sung the length of Beale Street. It's even been suggested that he wrote "Mr. Crump," but it was an old song, and it's unlikely that a Hernando bluesman would have made up a song to perform on his occasional trips to Memphis. When W.C. Handy described writing "Memphis Blues" he talked about another song called "Mister Crump," which he says was the basis for "Memphis Blues," and it was probably one of the versions of this that was the root source for Stokes' song. Stokes seems to have been well known on the medicine show circuit, as well as for his street singing, and in the summer of 1927, with Dan Sane, he did his first recording. They did seven titles for Paramount as the Beale Street Sheiks. The titles reflected the kind of near-minstrel material they were doing—"Beale Town Bound," "Jazzin' the Blues," "Half Cup of Tea"—but Stokes had a rich blues voice, and there were none of the minstrel show mannerisms in the way they played. It's difficult to say how they got up to Chicago to record, since Paramount didn't have much contact with Memphis. It was the largest blues company going at the time, and often singers went up on their own to audition; so they could have gotten with the company that way.

There seemed to be some interest in what they were doing at Paramount and they were in Chicago to record again the next month. Two of the pieces they did were remakes of things they'd done the month before, but at the same time they did three new pieces, including "Mr. Crump Don't Like It" and a "Blues in D." A friend from the medicine shows was up at the same time, Gus Cannon, who was recording for Paramount with Blind Blake. Paramount didn't follow up with them, however, and the next session was for Ralph Peer, who came into town in February 1928 to record the Memphis Jug Band. On February 1 Frank and Dan did four titles, including their brilliant "Downtown Blues," which was released on Vic 21272. They were in the improvised studio in the McCall Building the same day that the Jug Band did "Snitchin' Gambler Blues" and "Evergreen Money Blues." The week had started for Peer with the first four pieces that Cannon recorded with his Jug Stompers.

The sound on the Victor sides was much better than on the Paramount recordings, and Stokes's compelling, almost harsh voice came through with immediate clarity, and their guitar duets were brilliantly exciting. The next summer he did two short sessions by himself, doing four songs on August 27, 1928, and two more the next day. Sane joined him again on August 30, and they did four more titles, including the fine "T'Ain't Nobody's Business If I Do, Part 1 and Part 2," which was rather popular for them. Peer was recording Furry Lewis at the same time, and Furry did his classic "Kassie Jones" the same day that Stokes returned for his second session, Tuesday August 28th. Stokes's two pieces were done in the middle of Furry's session. The next year he recorded again, both for Paramount, with Dan Sane again as the Beale Street Sheiks, and for Victor. The Paramount sessions were done in Chicago in March 1929, and Victor recorded him in Memphis in September. These sessions were his last and he played without Sane. On six of the songs he used Will Batts on violin, but for his final two blues, on September 30, he played alone again, recording pieces with evocative titles, "Frank Stokes' Dream" and "Memphis Rounders Blues."

In the three years that Frank Stokes was a recording artist he did thirty-nine songs—a large number for the time and more than someone like Robert Johnson was able to do seven years later. He wasn't an imaginative singer—his style was simple and direct, and his texts were usually assemblages of familiar local verses. In their simplicity his texts matched his singing style.

> Now listen baby, I want to come back home.
> Now listen baby, I want to come back home.
> Then I'll tell you what happen, baby, since your man been gone.

There was a kind of flat literalness in his songs, and there was little use of complex imagery.

> I ain't no rounder, but I stays at home,
> I mean I ain't no rounder, but I stays at home.
> If you don't like my treatment you sure can leave me alone.
>
> Baby, someday you'll come to be my friend.
> Baby, someday you'll come to be my friend.
> Then we'll be alright, be back on the road again. . . .

But there was something that Stokes and Sane had that gave their blues their fresh excitement and their sauntering nonchalance. The verse could be something like:

> Hey listen mama, the world is done gone away,
> Hey listen mama, the world is done gone away,
> I got a bad luck deal give me trouble every day

sung in Frank's heavy voice, but behind the words he and Dan were playing some of the most marvelous two-guitar ragtime duets ever to get onto record. And it wasn't just for one or two songs—they did it on piece after piece. Sometimes, as in "Hunting Blues," the two guitars had a little of the sound that Henry Thomas had in his guitar part for "Fishing Blues," but most of what they did can't really be compared with anything else. Garfield Akers and Joe Calicott, who had known Frank when they were first starting out, did guitar duets with some of the complexity of Stokes and Sane, but they were doing music that had developed out of the field holler forms, and it had a more ambiguous harmonic structure. What Stokes and Sane were playing wasn't the kind of classic ragtime of Scott Joplin, but it had its own excited exuberance.

Most of their songs were blues, even if there were minstrel show elements woven in. Some were ragtime songs, and the verses fit the relaxed rhythm of their fingers.

I never never never
Can forget that day
When you called me baby,
How long, how long.
I ain't had no lovin'
How long, how long

Have you seen my baby baby baby
Tell her hurry home
I ain't no good baby,
How long, how long.
And I'm on my way, babe,
How long, how long.

In their accompaniments Frank took the simple rhythm, though he used changing c h o r d positions to give his playing more variety. Around this Dan wove a loose, syncopated line, sometimes melodic, sometimes harmonic. Sometimes he emphasized what Frank was doing—and there would be a moment of strutting rhythm as both of them picked out a bass lick—and sometimes he wove a filigree around it, as if he was so pleased with what Frank was doing that he didn't want to get in the way. All of their recordings had verses left open for the guitars; on some, like "Rockin' on the Hill Blues," they played verse after verse of pure country ragtime, without a vocal. It was the kind of music that people had to dance to—they couldn't keep their feet still. A musician named Lincoln Jackson —who played the second part with Frank when Frank came out to his little town of Cordova, outside of Memphis,—remembered this kind of irresistible rhythm as an integral part of Frank's style, and he told Bengt Olsson:

   . . . *In them days we had what you call moonlight picinics, you know.*
   They'd last for three days straight! Out in the woods, you know; lots

of shade and ain't no one goin' bother you out there. People came in buggies or horseback from miles around. In the night we'd light rags with oil so everything'd be fine . . . barbecued hogs, goats an' chicken; had lots of moonshine whiskey an' crap games. Man, we had ourselves a time! That's the kind o' occasion Frank'd play for us. Sometimes we had drum and fife bands playin' all 'em marches an' stuff, but everyone was jus' wild 'bout string music. Frank sure could make 'em do the Charleston 'n' Shim Sham Shimmy! He had a good rhythm, you know. I'd second him most of the time—we were pretty close; he'd stay at my place every time he came aroun'."

This is what you hear in the irresistible guitar duets that Frank and Dan recorded. If you can just imagine dancing along with it a little you can get the feel of a country picnic and a smoky fire cooking the barbecue, and the taste of homemade liquor still burning your tongue, and people around you picking up their feet and dancing. Sometimes couples dancing, sometimes a man doing his own buck dance to show off a little, sometimes a woman dancing alone with a baby in her arms, the baby's laughter joining in the enthusiasm.

The Depression finished recording for Frank, though he went on playing for years afterward. Dan took part in one more group of recordings, the sessions that Jack Kelly did in New York on August 1, 2, and 3, 1933, with three or four of the Beale Street regulars, including Will Batts, as the South Memphis Jug Band. In 1930 Frank was living with his father again not far from Will Batts's house. Willie Borum played with Frank and his son Roosevelt when they went out on the streets in the late thirties. Frank was living on Carnes Avenue at this time, and there was a daughter, Georgia, as well as a son. He was an old man now, though he kept traveling and playing a little. He seems to have left his wife and gone back to Mississippi, and he died in Clarksdale about 1960. He is said to have eaten meat accidentally sprinkled with DDT in the Snow Cafe on Esaquina Street. A woman, Viola Miller, said that her man used to play with Frank when he would come down to Clarksdale, even though mostly he was there to pick cotton. She was the one who described his death by poisoning, although no death certificate has been found. But she remembered his music. "He had a heavy voice and played with a heavy beat." That was Frank Stokes.

7.
Some Singers Outside of Memphis

If someone wanted to get to Brownsville he had to go east, away from downtown Memphis, then when the highways divided he had to stay on Route 79—the right-hand road. The left-hand road—Route 51—led up north through Henning and Ripley. All of them were as much east as north of Memphis, country towns in the rolling, tree-covered land that had been cleared down to its yellowred soil, then planted in cotton and soybeans. The soybeans are recent; when the land was first cleared it was all used for cotton, with a little space left around the cabins for vegetables, some of the land left for a few rows of corn. On the hillsides and back in the ravines there is a heavy growth of trees and brush, and on a fall day, walking back along the fences under the shadows of the trees, you kick away piled oak leaves, as deep brown as the dirt under them. You can smell smoke from cabin fires—through the lowering light a man walks ahead of you with his shotgun and his dog, doing a little hunting while there's still some light.

West Tennessee wasn't like the Delta, only 65 or so miles to the south. It didn't have a concentrated black farm population; it didn't have the crowding and the isolation of the Delta shack communities. The musicians coming out of the small towns and off the farms tended to drift into Memphis and become part of the rough crowd of singers and bluesmen working along Beale Street. But there was a country tradition, a style for all of them to draw on, even if it wasn't clearly identifiable—like the Mississippi bottleneck style, or the guitar rhythms of the Texas men. Most of them finger-picked the guitar, with the kind of loose raggy feel on the uptempo pieces that Frank Stokes and Dan Sane had. On the slower blues they often chorded behind the vocal phrase, then filled in the measure after it with small runs on the upper strings. There wasn't a lot of the unison guitar-voice melodies that were used in the Delta. If a slide or a bottleneck was used it was for a special piece—like "John Henry." The singing was also lighter in texture, the voices pitched higher, and the tone shaped farther forward in the mouth. It was a vocal tone a step closer toward a country white intonation. Often there was some uncertainty in the vocal phrase and the dominant phrase was anticipated by an upward tone shift that was slightly awkward.

Not all of the men that came into town stayed in Memphis. They liked life better back in the small towns where they'd grown up. One of the singers that Willie Borum played with a lot in the thirties was a guitarist and singer from Henning named Allen Shaw. They went to New York on September 17 and 18, 1934. Shaw is remembered as a tall man by the people in Henning that Bengt Olsson talked to, tall and well-built. Willie Borum just remembers that he was always traveling; there was no way to keep up with him. He had a job in Memphis when Willie met him, but he never stayed long on any job. He was a skilled guitarist, but his playing didn't have a strong individuality, and of the five blues he recorded only two were issued, "I Couldn't Help it" and "Moanin' the Blues" on Vocalion 02844. He played a lot with Noah Lewis when Noah was living in Henning, and in the late thirties he was more or less settled down in the small farm town, working at the C.S.O. Rice cotton gin. He died in Henning in 1940, at about the age of fifty.

These towns weren't very far out of Memphis. About forty-five miles. Noah Lewis could come in to work with Cannon, then go back up to Ripley or Henning the next day. In Memphis Noah was always with people like Cannon or Willie Borum—who learned how to play the harp with help from Noah—but in the country he worked at little grocery stores, or for picnics or dances. He's remembered in 1925 at a store called Orysa just outside of Henning with a guitar player named Jim Garrison. Many guitar players filled in with him, including Norman Haliburton and Cordelius Treadway. Eddie Green told Bengt Olsson:

> I played with Noah here in Henning. We had a band. I played guitar and Allen Shaw was in the band too. Occasionally Son Green played in the band. We played songs like "Joe Turner," "Big Fat Woman," "Casey Jones," "C. C. Rider" and others. I remember when we played at Cherry. A woman came in at a party and found her boyfriend with another woman. She grabbed Son's box and hit the boyfriend over the head, busting the guitar, and got the strings hung under his nose and ears! On another occasion my girl slapped me with a pocketbook. I hit her over the head with my guitar. On the Crutcher farm we had a party that lasted two days. There were many fights but the party never ceased. They just kept on drinking, playing and fighting. . . .

Noah had a son in Ripley who also was named Noah and played the harmonica. He'd lost his wife after they'd moved to Ripley, and his son died in Ripley as well. He stayed on in Ripley through the years that he was recording, just going down to rehearse with Cannon before they had to go into the studio. His life went on after the sessions, and he stayed up in the country, in the last years working as a farmhand for Willie Smith at Henning. It wasn't far from where he'd been born about 1890. His music stayed as pure and as expressive for years—and the people around Henning and Ripley still remember the sound of his harmonica. But in the last years he was in poor health, he couldn't play, and he was living in a small shack outside of town. It was under a large tree, a wood building with a narrow door, a windowless front, a board step out into the weeds. He was still there in 1960 when he died. He lost his way, was out all night, and was nearly frozen when he was found. His feet were amputated at the hospital, but he couldn't be saved, and he died in the hospital in Ripley.

Brownsville was on the other highway leading out of Memphis, but there were dirt roads going back and forth between Ripley and Henning and Brownsville, and all the singers knew each other. Brownsville's larger than the other two, and it had its own musical life in the twenties and thirties. It had its younger musicians like Hammie Nixon, who played harp, and Yank Rachel, who played mandolin. It had its younger blues singers, Charlie Pickett and "Brownsville" Son Bonds, who made recordings in the thirties. For Pickett there were only two sessions, August 2 and 3, 1937, but Son Bonds had three sessions in 1934, one in 1938, and a last in 1941. He wasn't a strong singer, but he had a commercial style and the songs he did were young but effective. He was a good guitarist and his voice had the usual rural Tennessee nasal sound. Pickett was more interesting as a singer, but he did only four blues. One of them, "Down the Highway," is almost free rhythmically, with the guitar playing in unison with the voice, then following with its own musical phrase. His voice is high and his singing is in a uniquely personal style. It is a startling blues—a suggestion of a country style that has had little representation on record and now is completely lost. But there is "Down the Highway"—first issued on a Decca single 7707—as a brilliant example of it.

But it was another singer who gave Brownsville its place in the blues, one of the greatest country bluesmen to record in the years of the Depression, Sleepy John Estes, who spent almost his entire life in the town.

Sleepy John Estes.

8.
Sleepy John Estes

I was raised in Lawdry County, you know I was schooled on Winfield Lane.
I was raised in Lawdry County, you know I was schooled on Winfield Lane.
You know what I made of myself, it's a cryin' shame.

It was a verse John Estes sang often in the first few months after he'd been found still living near Brownsville, Tennessee. It was his flat, hard comment on the reality of the years he'd spent there, living in a harsh poverty that was deeply disturbing to see. Winfield Lane was a rutted, unpaved farm road running through the red-brown clay earth outside of Brownsville, Tennessee. Most of the farms had been abandoned and there was only a scattering of houses along the road, some of them deserted cabins with fallen-in roofs and peeling tar paper. There were small stretches of cotton, some grazing land, but most of the land was overgrown with brush and trees. The cabin John lived in was about a mile and a half from the turn into Brownsville, a sagging wood shack that had once been painted red. The ground in front of it was bare of grass, an open mud space with a refuse of dirty dishes, old clothes, a chair that had gotten broken and left outside the door. It had only two rooms, one of them empty except for a bundle of rags on the filth of the floor, the other room with a chair, a rusted wood stove, and two beds piled with the same rags that were on the floor of the other room. A metal plate with bits of food stuck to it had been left on the chair, and flies clustered around the rest of the dishes left in a bucket on the floor. There was no electricity or water. In the daytime most of the light came in through the cracks between the cabin's warped planks. It looked like any of the abandoned cabins left in the fields, but John Estes was living in it, with his wife and five small children.

Many of the old bluesmen who were found still living in the 1950s and 1960s were living in ghetto buildings, or in shabby houses in small towns in the South, but Estes's poverty had a desperateness to it. He'd long been troubled with his eyes, and he'd finally become completely blind. Even knowing that he was in poor health, blind, and living in a poor shack, I still wasn't prepared for the sight of him, a gaunt, tall figure in dirty farm clothes, a shapeless straw hat on his head, sitting alone on a bare wooden chair in front of the cabin of a neighbor. Because he'd been told someone wanted to see him, he had an old guitar across his lap, the strings rusted, a pencil tied around the neck as a kind of capo. One of his sons, who was about nine years old, led him back and forth from his house to the Meaux house, and it was painful to watch him stumbling along, holding his guitar, his feet scuffing with uncertainty over the dirt and stones.

A few months later John was able to move into Brownsville, and with the earnings that came in from concerts and recordings he was able to add to the welfare check he received from the state of Tennessee, but the years of darkness and poverty on the country road left their marks on both his health and his spirit. The man across the road, a sharecropper with a family of his own to feed, had tried to do what he could for John, but he felt that it was John's blindness that had left him so helpless. "People cheats him, you know, when he goes and buys things. If he gets some butter they makes him pay four times what it says on the counter; then they don't give him his right change." He had grown blind when he was older, and he hadn't developed any of the ways to deal with his blindness that someone younger learns. He was only fifty-eight years old, that afternoon at the cabin on Winfield Lane—but he looked and moved like a man in his seventies.

A handful of the bluesmen of the twenties seemed to sum up the intense emotionalism and strong musicality of this early blues period, when it was a music of unique individuality and a clearly sensed personal expression. It was not blues bands or groups, or the interplay of one instrumentalist with another. All of that was to come later. In the twenties it was still largely a music coming from the country to the city—it was still a music of singers living in small communities and functioning as the expression—and the entertainment—of the people in these communities. Of the hundreds of blues singers who recorded during this period, Estes was one of the most individual. During a time when there were many great blues artists, he was one of the greatest. It was his way of using his materials that gave Estes his greatness. Many singers were using the same verses, many had used the melodies, and the forms he used were generally clearly within the blues idiom of the period he was recording—but he was like a stream from the farm country where he grew up. It picks up its materials from the banks that it washes against; then it leaves them farther downstream spread out in new patterns and arrangements.

John was born John Adam Estes—friends in Brownsville still call him John Adam—in Lauderdale County, outside of Ripley. It comes out as "Lawdry" when he sings about it. He was born on January 25, 1904, one of sixteen children. His father was a sharecropper and played a little music. John started on his father's guitar when he was still a child. When he was eleven they moved into Brownsville, in 1915, and he did get a little time in school in a wood frame school building on Winfield Lane, not far from where he was living when he was found. About this time he was hit in the eye with a stone in a baseball game and he was never able to see well again. He worked a little in the fields along with the rest of his brothers and sisters. This was still the old farm life of the rural South. Cotton all year around, with its hours of digging and chopping and weeding and picking. John didn't like field work, and when his father died in 1920 he started making his living with his music. It wasn't much of a living, just the usual country picnics and parties, playing for dances. Long hours sweating in the lantern light, singing the blues until his voice was gone and he couldn't do much more than strum the guitar. Memphis wasn't far, but he didn't come in. He wasn't an entertainer, and he wasn't a street singer. He had his own blues, and he had his own life in the small town where he'd grown up.

Brownsville, like most small towns in the South, had its little square, its courthouse, its line of one-story shops looking hopefully at the courthouse for any sign of business. Their plate-glass windows were filled with cheap watches and cotton dresses, kitchen utensils, lanterns, car parts, and tools. It also had a few other musicians. John was soon playing with James Rachel—who was usually known as Yank and had been in Brownsville all of his life. He was younger than John—four years younger. He was born on March 16, 1908. He learned the guitar from his uncle, Daniel Taylor, but he was also a brilliant mandolin player, and it was the mandolin that he played with John. They met at a party where John was playing, and, though Yank had managed to get through the sixth grade in school, he didn't see any kind of job he could do in Brownsville and he drifted into music. The other musician closely associated with Brownsville and John is his harmonica player, Hammie Nixon. He was nine years younger than John, and he was only fourteen the first time they met. He was born in January 1913 in Ripley and he grew up playing the harmonica. "I don't know when I started. I just played it since I was a kid." John heard him at a country supper and got his mother to let him live in Brownsville. And they've been close friends ever since.

The years in Brownsville before he recorded gave John's music its individuality. He was a great singer, with a high, thin, crying voice that had almost a child's despair—but he wasn't much worried about the guitar, and he depended on the musicians with him to give his songs their final structure. Yank was with him on his first sessions—Hammie was too young—but when he began recording again five years later Hammie was with him too. His harmonic ideas were so loosely developed that it was only musicians who knew his style that could really work with him. Hammie knew his music so well that he could play a harp line almost in unison with John's voice, and Yank had worked out a complicated mandolin style to go with John's strummed guitar rhythms. John was twenty-five when he came into Memphis and auditioned for Ralph Peer and did his first session on September 16, 1929, during an extended field trip that Victor made during that month to record the Memphis Jug Band, Cannon's Jug Stompers, and Frank Stokes.

Estes worked with one of the Memphis Jug Band men, Jab Jones, on his first Victor sessions, and he knew the songs well enough to record versions of some of the jug band songs later, but he was something that they weren't. He was a country bluesman in the classic sense. His music had come out of the field singing and the country breakdowns of the countryside around Brownsville, and he was able to build a creative structure—the way a person builds a house—out of the materials of his life.

John Estes—"Sleepy John Estes" as he was called on record labels, because he'd gone off to sleep on the little bandstand at a country dance and his friends started calling him "Sleepy"—was to have a long, and eventually successful, recording career in the years between 1929 and 1941, even if his life in Brownsville wasn't changed much by it. When he did go to record he was gone only a few days—at most a few weeks. There wasn't much money for the sessions—someone as successful as Memphis Minnie was getting only $12.50 for every side she recorded, and that was a flat rate. Any royalties had to come from compositions. Hammie Nixon recorded ten songs as accompanist for Little Buddy Doyle on a session for Vocalion in Memphis in 1939 and his total payment for the session was $10. If any Chicago musicians remembered John they remembered him as one of the Southern bluesmen who came in town, made some sides, spent the money, and got back home as best they could. With the amounts of money he was making it wouldn't have taken him long to go through it, and he sings about riding freight trains and jumping off at hobo jungles with a depressing sense of reality.

In the twelve years that he made records in his early period he recorded forty-four blues for first Victor label, then Decca, and finally Victor's lower-priced label Bluebird. At his final session, on September 24, 1941, he recorded first with two Brownsville musicians, Son Bonds and Raymond Thomas, as The Delta Boys. They did six songs, including "When the Saints Go Marchin' In" and "Every Time My Heart Beats." Later the same day John recorded three blues, "Lawyer Clark Blues," "Little Laura Blues," and "Working Man Blues." Thomas again played imitation string bass, but Son Bonds had switched from kazoo to guitar. John's first Memphis session, on September 16, 1929, was more of an audition than a session. The engineers did only one song, "Broken-Hearted, Ragged and Dirty Too," and it was left as an unissued test. He had Yank Rachel with him, and Yank worked well with him, but Jab Jones, the pianist, was working with the Memphis Jug Band and he probably wasn't familiar enough with John's individual rhythmic style. They came back in the studio eight days later and this time—on September 24—they got a usuable song, the fine version of the "Goin' to Brownsville" melody that was titled, probably for copyright purposes, "The Girl I Love, She Got Long Curly Hair."

They seem to have recorded slowly, and they didn't get more than two songs a day at any of the sessions. They came back two days later and got two of their best blues recorded, a second version of "Broken-Hearted, Ragged and Dirty Too " and "Diving Duck Blues." There was a last session for the year the next week, on October 2, but Jab had dropped out and there was a harmonica player added. They again got only a single blues, "Black Mattie Blues," The next May Victor was in Memphis again and they got the three of them together—Jab back on piano—for four different sessions. The first day, May 13, they got

"Milk Cow Blues" and "Street Car Blues." May 17 they recorded again, but this time Yank Rachel did the singing on the first song, "Expressman Blues." Four days later there was another two-song session, this time with John singing; then Jab dropped out again and there were four songs recorded on May 30, two of them with Yank singing. Victor 23318 was released with two of Yank's vocals—the "Expressman Blues" and 'Sweet Mama"—but John was listed on the label as the singer, and for some time the different voices with the same name caused a little confusion.

The Depression deepened after the last Victor sessions, and John's life in Brownsville went on pretty much the way it had before. He went on playing the little picnics and the auctions and dances—a thin, withdrawn man who played his guitar with a kind of repetitive loping rhythm and sang with a kind of emotional possession. Hammie Nixon was working with him, and they managed to keep something going. Gennett Records had tried to continue their race label with a cheap series called Champion, but the early thirties were too hard for them to get through. They sold the copyright for Champion in June 1935 to the new Decca label. John and Hammie had been going up to Chicago for occasional trips, trying to play their blues and trying to get another session, and for a period after 1931 they stayed in the city. Big Bill Broonzy, whose memory was colorful, if not entirely reliable, described a blues contest between himself and Memphis Minnie, with John and Richard M. Jones as the judges. They decided Minnie had won it and carried her around the room on their shoulders, while Bill walked off with the prize, a bottle of whiskey. If it did happen it would have been sometime during this period that John was in the North. He managed to get to know Mayo Williams, who went from Vocalion to the new Decca series, and it was for Decca that John recorded again, two sessions with Hammie, done in Chicago on July 9 and July 17, 1935. Their first release, "Down South Blues" and "Stop That Thing," was the first release on the new Champion race series—it was Champion 50001, and all three records that they did came out first on Champion. But the 5000 series wasn't strong enough, and all of the releases were moved over to Decca's very successful 7000 series.

But it still wasn't time for John to reach his audience. The Champion releases were loose, surging blues, but they were on the wrong label. It wasn't until he recorded for Decca again in 1937 that he began to get a solid popularity. He did eighteen blues in three sessions in 1937 and 1938, then six more in 1940, and the next year he was recording for Victor's very popular Bluebird line. It was only the Musicians Union's ban on recording and the wartime shellac shortage that ended his early career. He was popular enough to have his photograph on the front of the "Decca Race Records" catalog, his face set and unsmiling, between the broadly grinning photos of Peetie Wheatstraw and Georgia White. Victor, to cash in on his popularity, even released some of the first recordings they've done with him in 1929 on their Bluebird series. It was a long, rather prolific, and successful recording career—and that made the poverty of the years afterward even more difficult to accept. Out of all the music that he recorded, all the songs he composed, there should have been something to keep him out of that crumbling cabin in the overgrown fields outside of Brownsville.

73

The blues that John recorded are a brilliant expression of the depth of the blues as a poetic expression. In his singing and in the songs that he wrote there is a complete expression of himself as a human being, a portrait of the people living around him, and an insistent commentary on the reality of life in western Tennessee in the shabby, dusty years of the Depression. It's possible to see—to understand—something of this life because of John's blues about it—because of his own unsentimental, clear-eyed understanding of it that he was able to express in the wistful reflection of his songs. He was one of the greatest singers of the early blues period—with a sensitive, intense voice that seemed almost to cry in its sadness and its ruefulness. It was a clear, high voice that was almost free of the limits of the blues verses and had its own sensed rhythms. It wasn't a sensual voice—John wasn't particularly concerned with physicality in his blues—but it was an emotional, powerful voice that hung in a fierce clarity over the sound of his guitar.

The form of his songs was on one level generally simple, and on another stubbornly complex. He usually worked within standard blues forms, but he kept placing them in a rhythmic context that forced the music into new, and often awkward, dimensions. The first sessions were remarkable for their rhythmic ambiguity. Because of his limitation as a guitarist, John had developed a kind of doubled rhythm that he strummed as he sang, using only simple melodic figures at the end of a vocal phrase. Yank had learned to play along with him by emphasizing the lyricism of his voice, and on the mandolin he played long melodic lines, interspersed with rhythmic elements that doubled John's strumming. Jones, playing the piano, was left in the difficult position of accompanying a voice that was singing in standard blues progressions, while the guitar was playing a simple strum in a kind of double time. He was able to work something out, and the tension between the two rhythms gave the best of their performances a rich, textured sound that moved in sudden emphasis under the directness of the voice.

John was to use the "Brownsville" melody for most of his recording career, but it's difficult to tell where he learned it. It had already been recorded before his version of it, and one of the recordings is very similar to his in the general shaping of the phrases—particularly the third phrase—and in the emotional "feel" of the voice. This version of it is a strange, clumsy recording by an accordion player and singer from—probably—Cleveland, Mississippi, named Walter Rhodes. Rhodes was a street singer who worked in small Mississippi towns like Cleveland and Bobo, but when he recorded for Columbia in 1927 there were two guitarists on the sessions with him. Their names were Maylon and Richard Harney, brothers from Arkansas who were called "Pet" and "Can" on the recording. Rhodes seems to be playing a simple, archaic kind of accompaniment on his accordion, which sounds like the kind of square, simple instruments that the Cajun musicians used, while the Harney brothers are attempting to play a fairly modern and skilled blues duet. No real rhythm emerges out of the jumble of styles, but it is possible to hear Rhodes voice, and his version of the melody is strong and effective.

Goin' to buy me a roos-ter___ put him in my back door. _

Goin' to buy me a roos-ter___ put him in my back door. _

See a stran-ger com-in' he lost his way be-fore.

Charley Patton also seems to have heard the record—or heard Rhodes—and he used it as the basis for his "Banty Rooster Blues" recorded two years later. Although it's difficult to follow the chord progression in Rhodes's recording, the harmony he is singing is a standard twelve-bar blues, though—from the inflection of the second phrase—he would seem to be singing in a modal scale rather than a diatonic. Also the rhythm of his version is regular—that is, within a standard twelve-bar, 4/4, form. In his first recording of it Estes's version is significantly different. It still has the initial introductory vocal tones—two beats before the beginning of each sung phrase—that were a carryover from the old phrasing of the field holler. But instead of a steady 4/4 beat there's a kind of suspended rhythmic jog—like a man running two steps in place—as the phrase picks up again. But in other respects the melody is very similar.

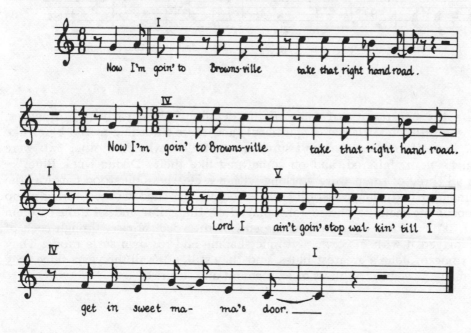

Now I'm goin' to Browns-ville take that right hand road.

Now I'm goin' to Browns-ville take that right hand road.

Lord I ain't goin' stop wal-kin' till I

get in sweet ma-ma's door. ___

75

John's vocal is in the purest holler tradition, and it would be as effective if he was walking on a dirt road singing it to himself—a way singers often had of letting their women know they were on their way in from the fields. The tension in the rhythm comes from Jab's efforts to sort out the involved relationship between the double strum of the guitar and the freely shifting melody of the voice and the mandolin. John essentially is singing in 4/4, while the accompaniment is in 8/8. Jab was forced to fill the space with considerably more piano than bluesmen of the twenties usually did, and the rhythmic complexity comes from his shifts of phrase and harmony. John's guitar is heard as an almost inaudible strumming in the lower strings.

The other songs from the first sessions were generally within the standard twelve-bar form, and it was only for this version of the "Brownsville" melody that John kept the holler phrasing. When he recorded it again more than thirty years later it still had this same structure. On one of the other songs, "Street Car Blues," the phrase length was irregular, as he added beats in his guitar strum to the line endings, but the other blues either had a twelve-bar form or were in a recitative form that kept the twelve-bar structure but used a doubled first line in a kind of recited vocal phrase. It's the same form that someone like Lightnin' Hopkins has used for dozens of blues. As John used it in his first sessions it was a clearly defined melodic root he used repeatedly for later blues.

Now look-y here, ba-by, see what you done done.
done made me love you, now yo' man done come, 'cause... Need more, etc.

Despite the uncertainty of some of the details of these early performances, they were in their own way magnificent, and there's nothing in the blues like them. Even if Jab Jones wasn't sure how to follow what the other two were doing, he never faltered, and on something like their "Diving Duck Blues"— when all three of them were working within a clearly understood pattern—the instrumental texturing was brilliantly effective. Jab had worked out a piano version of the melodic phrase John played on the guitar and all three of them played it in a kind of unison at the end of the vocal phrase, though each of them played it with his own rhythmic shading and his own scale mode. They were some of John's greatest blues, and they still, after all the years since they were made, have the freshness of excitement and surprise.

Brownsville, even though it is a small town, is on a major highway—it has radios and records. Whatever was going on in the blues made its way to Brownsville's flat, drab black section, and even John's music showed some of the changes as the years passed. It wasn't John's singing or Hammie's harmonica playing— it was the young musicians from Brownsville who recorded with them that made most of the change. John has had the same style for most of his life, and his guitar playing hasn't changed since his first days in the studio, but his recordings seem to have more variety—because of the different sound of his accompaniment and his slight adjustment of vocal rhythm and phrasing to the new sound. It was only on the first six sides for Champion—in the summer of 1935 when he and Hammie were in Chicago—that he was his own accompanist, and it's clear that he needed other musicians with him. He had found a kind of jogging, dancelike strum for his songs, and often there seemed to be almost no rhythmic connection between his voice and the accompaniment. The songs were exciting—with his voice at its most emotional, and the texts brilliant blues poems. Some of the best of his recitative blues were from these sessions—the fine "Drop Down Baby," with its refrain:

Well, my mama she don't 'low me to fool 'round all night long.
Now I may look like I'm crazy,
But poor John do know right from wrong

and his "Someday Baby," which influenced some of the Chicago singers when it was released the same year. But in a simple blues, like "Married Woman Blues," the limitations of his guitar playing begin to interfere with the effectiveness of the performance. He used his same strum for the blues, but in a more usual 4/4 tempo. The strum was unobstrusive, in itself, and his singing was always stunning enough to overcome the clumsiness of the background, but the harmonic structure of his playing was always uncertain. He seemed undecided as to how he wanted to play the simple tonic, subdominant, dominant harmonies that he was singing. Instead of the usual chord pattern of

I - I - I - I (sometimes IV for the second measure)
IV - IV - I - I
V - IV - I - I (or the V chord was held through the second measure)

John sometimes began with a measure of tonic and subdominant, two beats of each, though his subdominant wasn't a definite IV chord, and he divided the measure sometimes with the kind of subdominant chord coming first, sometimes second. His dominant chord in the last phrase was often used only for a single beat—not long enough to establish the harmony, but sudden enough to throw off the harmonic movement of the piece. After the beat—or two beats— he hurriedly went back to his little rhythmic strumming on his basic open chord. The guitarists who worked with him later—the Brownsville musicians Charlie Pickett and Son Bonds—sometimes found themselves haplessly following along, and there is some of the same confusion in their duets, with the guitars beginning a verse with the harmonic changes for the second line of the verse. The uncertainties of the guitar work wouldn't have been so obvious if John hadn't been so effective as a singer. He *sang* all the harmonic changes for the standard progressions—he just didn't bother to play them. And as a singer he was so brilliantly effective that for his best recordings the inadequacies of the accompaniment seem to be wholly wound into the texture of the song. On one of his late sessions, June 4, 1940, for Decca, the guitarist on some of the pieces sounds like another musician and there's a startling modernity in songs like "Jailhouse Blues." With its careful, melodic guitar work it's a recording that could have been made in the mid-1950s, and it emphasizes the effect that John's music had on the development of the blues in the years before the war.

It wasn't only as a singer that John Estes made a place for himself in the history of the blues. The verses he wrote have a directness and an immediacy that few singers can match. He could write the simple blues love songs that most of the singers of the thirties wrote by the hundreds, but he had much more on his mind. He had seen much more, and he wanted to tell about it. He had some of Patton's involvement with the place he lived in, and the people of Brownsville find their way into his blues—as people, not as symbols or standard blues types he's given a name. His blues about the mechanic Vassie Williams, who had a garage in nearby Durhamville, was a song about somebody he knew, somebody he was close to.

> Now Vassie can line your wheels, you know poor Vassie
>   can tune your horn.
> Now he can line your wheels, you know poor Vassie
>   can tune your horn
> Then when he set it out on the highway you can hear
>   your motor hum.
>
> Now my generator is bad, and you know my lights done stopped.
> Now my generator is bad, and you know my lights done stopped.
> And I reckon I'd better take it over to Durhamville, and I'm goin'
>   to stop at Vassie Williams' shop.

Sometimes he changed the names, but you can hear him mention the grocer Pat Mann and his son, who was a lawyer; another lawyer, Mr. Clark, had a whole song; most of the Brownsville police force comes in at one time or another; and even the mortician Al Rawls turns up in a song, as well as the local liquor store owner Peter Albert. As he said in one blues:

> Now Brownsville is my home, and you know I ain't goin'
>   to throw her down.
> Now Brownsville is my home, and you know I ain't goin'
>   to throw her down.
> Because I'm 'quainted with John Law, and they won't let me down.

His songs had this sense of a place and people, and he could write a blues that had the kind of details you hear in a country story. He had the literalness of Bukka White, but he had a stronger narrative sense, and in some of his blues you could follow what he was singing almost as a story, even if it wasn't a ballad song in the usual sense.

Now when I left Chicago I left on the G & M
Now when I left Chicago I left on that G & M
Then after I reach my home I had to change over on that L & N.

Now came in on that main west, and I put it down at Chicago Heights.
Now when I came in on that main west I put it down at Chicago Heights.
Now you know then poor John gone, and that's why I stayed all night.

Now if you hobo through Brownsville you better not be peepin' out.
Now if you hobo through Brownsville you better not be peepin' out.
Mr. Winn will get you and Mr. Guy Hare will wear you out.

Now out east from Brownsville it's about four miles from town.
Now out east from Brownsville it's about four miles from town.
Now if you ain't got your fare that's where they will let you down.

One of his songs was a personal ballad about a near drowning, the well-known "Floating Bridge," and in his description of what happened and then his song about it there's a clear illustration of the immediate relationship between his life and his music. As he told me:

I was travelin' in Hickman, Kentucky, and the car went in the high water, the '37 flood it was. Got going to my cousin's home and had to go across one of them floating bridges tied to the cable there, you know, to keep it from floating away, and we got on that bridge and hit that pretty rough, you know, the way he was driving. He lost control of the car and it went off to the left. I was sitting on the far side putting some strings in my shoes and I was the last one. There's two-three on the other side of me and that made me last getting out on the bridge.

Well, my cousin, it knocked him in the head scuffling in the car. He cut hisself and he's sitting up there on a log and he asks, "Everybody out?" "Unun, John's still in there." By that time I had come up the third time. He jumped off that board and saved me. He got me and put me under his arm and treaded water up to the bridge and pulled me up on to it.

Out of this John selected the details that were the most emotionally vivid for him and set them to the old melody usually known as "Two White Horses in a Line." He recorded it the next summer, August 2, 1937, in New York.

Now I never will forget that floating bridge.
(three times)
Tell me five minutes time in the water I was hid.

When I was going down I throwed up my hands.
(three times)
Please take me on dry land.

Now they carried me in the house and they laid me 'cross the bank.
(three times)
'Bout a gallon and a half of muddy water I had drank.

They dried me off and they laid me in the bed.
(three times)
Couldn't hear nothing but muddy water running through my head.

Now my mother often taught me quit playing a bum.
(three times)
Go somewhere, settle down and make a crop.

Now the people standing on the bridge was screaming and crying.
(three times)
Lord have mercy while we gwine.

It was in details like "Couldn't hear nothing but muddy water running through my head" that his blues found some of their greatest power.

John had also the rare ability to find sudden images, small phrases, that left an immediate impression of what he was trying to suggest in his song. He had phrases like "Now, went upstairs to pack my leaving trunk . . ." giving a complete sense of leaving, packing up, getting out, in the simple "leaving trunk." The verse goes on with a more obvious but still strong phrase, "I never had no whiskey; blues done made me sloppy drunk." He could give a whole sense of a crowded town and a loose Saturday's confusion in a phrase like "Now, I know the people is on a wander everywhere." And he summed up a woman in one of his most striking phrases, "Some of these women sure do make me tired, got a handful of 'gimme,' got a mouthful of 'much obliged.'" He had the poetic range to describe a relationship in simple but direct emotional terms:

Now asked sweet mama, let me be her kid.
She said, "I might, but I like to keep it hid."
Well, she looked at me, she begin to smile,

Says, "I thought I would use you for my man awhile.
Just don't let my husband catch you there,
Just don't let my husband catch you there."

And in another blues he could give the government advice on how to end the Depression.

Now you ought to cut off so many trucks and tractors, white folks,
    you ought to work more mules and men.
Now you ought to cut off so many trucks and tractors, white folks,
    you ought to work more mules and men.
Then you know that would make, ooh babe, money get thick again.

He was one of the strongest and most effective of the blues poets of the twenties and thirties, and some of his most striking phrases and images have become part of the language of the modern blues song.

It was Big Bill's book that stopped people from looking for John. Bill said that Estes had been a very old man when he recorded and that he'd been dead for years. Bill was actually eleven years older than Estes, so it's unlikely that he ever saw him at all, but John's singing style had such a unique, quavering quality to it that he sometimes did sound like an old man on his recordings. But other musicians knew of him and occasionally they mentioned him. In 1957 Big Joe Williams told Robert Koester, who owned Delmark Records and operated the Jazz Record Market in Chicago, "Sure, Sleepy John's still alive. He lives on a farm outside Brownsville, Tennessee." Koester hadn't known Big Joe long enough to sort out from what he said what was true and what was clearly not true. In 1959, when his shop was on South Wabash, a man working next door said, "My name is Sam Estes from Tennessee," but Koester thought he was making a kind of joke on the name Sleepy John Estes, and it wasn't until years later that he learned it was John's brother. It was finally Memphis Slim who led to John. He'd heard about him from Big Joe, and when he was asked by a young filmmaker, David Blumenthal, if he knew of any old bluesmen in that part of Tennessee, Slim told him to look for Estes. Blumenthal was making a film documenting some aspects of the new black freedom movement under the title *Citizen South, Citizen North*. He went to Brownsville, found the ruined shack where John was living, filmed it, and came back to Chicago. When he got back to town he decided he should film a modern jazz group in a nightclub, and he was sent to one of Koester's employees, Joe Segal, who knew a lot about the Chicago jazz scene. Joe talked to Blumenthal for a minute, then he went upstairs to get Koester. "Bob, there's a guy downstairs who claims he's located a blues singer named Sleepy John Estes."

Within a few weeks John was in Chicago for a first short tour. Koester had called a man named Odell Saunders who answered, "If I had known you were going to call I would have had John Estes stay around here—he was here an hour ago." Koester went down to Brownsville, immediately bought John some clothes—"slack britches" as his neighbor Phil Meux recalled—helped him get a guitar, and arranged to bring him up north. Since then he has managed John's business affairs, handled his recording sessions, and done what he could to help John find his way out of the poverty of the years when he was living on Winfield Lane. There was a second film documentary done a few weeks after John returned from his first trip. He and his family were still living in their cabin and I was able to film them there for *The Blues* in the early summer of 1962. It was stifling and hot, and it wasn't possible to work in the heat for more than a few moments at a time. John sat stilly through it all, his eyes closed, his face without expression. The children moved around him a little, but they were almost as silent, and for a sequence of the family on the porch they sat almost without movement, the sun glaring on the hard-packed dirt in front of them, the boards of the porch squeaking if anybody shifted from one foot to another.

At the Newport Folk Festival in 1964 John was as silent as he had been in the Tennessee sunlight. Many young blues enthusiasts milling around behind the stage area before he sang almost missed seeing him. He was in a jacket and slacks, wearing a shirt and tie. He had on an ordinary businessman's hat and he was wearing dark glasses. There was some of the same reserve when he sang, but Hammie Nixon, as always, was with him, and Hammie's stubby figure filled the stage as he went from harmonica to jug, doing his best to keep the crowd entertained. Yank Rachel was with them as well. He'd been found living in Indianapolis and he'd also begun recording for Koester's Delmark label. The three of them seemed a little unsure of themselves, on a low stage in Newport's steady gray drizzle, playing for a large crowd—almost four thousand people watched their afternoon workshop appearances—that was scattered across the grass in blue jeans and sweat shirts. But the music was still there—the cry was still in John's voice—and their songs were a moving glimpse of the world of Brownsville, and the people who lived in it, thirty years before. It was all there, in the blues that John Estes had built out of the simple materials of his life.

I been go-in' cra-zy— I just can't help my-self.—

Uu-uum-uuh-umm. I'm go-in' cra-zy I just can't help my-self.—

Uu-uum-uuh-uum. Be-cause the man I'm lo-vin'

he love that some-one else.—

(See page 90.)

9. Memphis Minnie

It is, of course, a misnomer to speak of the country blues artists as "bluesmen" since there was a scattering of women who played and sang the blues throughout the South, but the masculine element in the country blues was so dominant, and the male singers so completely identified with the style, that the term "bluesmen" is very useful. The generalization of the urban blues in the early period as dominated by women and the country blues by men holds generally true, despite occasional exceptions. There was no male singer who was as significant in the urban blues scene as Bessie Smith, Ma Rainey, Clara Smith, Ida Cox, or Sara Martin, just as, in the country blues, there was no woman singer with the influence of Lonnie Johnson, Lemon Jefferson, Leroy Carr, or Big Bill. This generalization, however, has to give way a little in the thirties, for in the middle of the masculine country blues world there was the exultantly feminine figure of Minnie McCoy, a handsome, vibrant woman known to the people who bought her records as "Memphis Minnie."

Her professional name is misleading in some ways, because for most of her career she—along with most of the other commercial blues artists—was living and working in Chicago, and a point could be made for excluding her from a discussion of regional blues styles. As the blues became more and more of a marketing phenomenon in the thirties, almost all of the regional groupings broke down in Chicago. But she had many years of playing in Memphis before she began recording, and even at the end of her career there was still a suggestion of the Memphis vocal tone and the kind of earnest rhythmic movement that was characteristic of that city's style. Also she was part of the Beale Street scene for many years, and it seems important to include her in a discussion of Memphis music, even if much of what she sang and played was done elsewhere and reflected many other influences.

Like nearly all of the city's blues artists, she wasn't born in Memphis, but unlike them—most were Mississippians—she was born farther south, in Algiers,

Memphis Minnie.

Louisiana, across the river from New Orleans, on June 3, 1896. Her family's name was Douglas, and she was the first of thirteen children. Her name was Minnie, but she was so active when she was young that her parents nicknamed her "Kid," and she was always known as Kid Douglas in her years in Memphis. When she was still young, only seven, her family moved to Walls, Mississippi, which is just over the Mississippi line, about fifteen miles southwest of Memphis on Highway 61; then a year later they moved into Memphis itself. Her first instrument was a banjo that she later remembered she learned to play in two weeks, and by the time she was fifteen she had gotten herself a guitar and was "serenading" along Beale Street.

She was part of the crowded, hectic life along Beale Street for nearly twenty years, usually playing and singing with a small group or with one of the local bluesmen. She was well known by all the singers and she seems to have learned most of their finger-picking techniques, as well as the blues and songs that were popular in the city. She was especially close to the musicians of the Memphis Jug Band and for some time lived with Will Weldon, who was one of the band's original members. By the late twenties, however, she was living with a Mississippi singer named Joe McCoy, and much of her early recording was done with him. She remembers that a scout for Columbia heard her singing in a barbershop and sent them to New York to the studios there. Ralph Peer seems to have missed her, even though he'd tried recording some other women singers on his trips away from New York. The interest was in male singers at this point, and even Columbia recorded only one song with Minnie singing and didn't release that for some time. Probably their pseudonyms of "Kansas Joe" and "Memphis Minnie" were given them by Frank Walker at Columbia, since she was still called Kid Douglas by the other Memphis musicians, and the people who remember Joe usually refer to him by his own name. His records were also released under the name Big Joe, Hallelujah Joe, Mud Dauber Joe, Georgia Pine Boy, and Mississippi Mudder; so there would seem to be a basic confusion as to his stylistic identity.

In some ways there is some of the same confusion in the music they were doing together in the late twenties since so many influences were present in the Memphis musical scene. Other people close to them were recording, including Will Weldon and the Jug Band, and many of the Mississippi singers with stylistic similarities to what Joe was doing were coming into Memphis to record; so there was a great deal of music to choose from. Everything seems to have made some impression on what they were playing on the streets, and certainly Minnie, by this time in her mid-thirties, was a completely assured performer. But this early Memphis period, even though it covered so many years of her life, is perhaps not so crucial in considering Minnie's career, since she became one of the most successful of the commercial performers of the next period of the blues.

It's difficult to make any assessment of the artistic development of a commercial singer like her. For one thing there are so many recordings, and in their larger patterns of expression they reflect more of a response to the popular blues market than they do any changing artistic attitudes. She was successful at the beginning because of her voice, her muscianship, and her songs, and she stayed successful by making changes in the music she was creating—changes which kept what she was doing closer to the line the blues was taking as a popular music. She was able to continue her career for almost twenty years, and if she had not suffered a stroke at the time when there was a new interest in the older blues artists she would have been performing and recording again. She made more than two hundred recordings, and they reflect almost every kind of blues that was popular in the thirties, from love songs, to the kind of party blues that the Mississippi Sheiks and Tampa Red were doing, to a raucous celebration of Joe Louis's success, "Joe Louis Strut." But it's still possible to trace a kind of overall pattern in her blues and to follow some of the techniques that led to her large success.

A popular music—and the thirties blues had certainly become a popular entertainment form—has to be clearly identifiable and on a larger level comprehensible. People have to be able to recognize it and understand it, which means it has to be simple. But its simplicity means that it can easily degenerate into a facile manipulation of the elements that are immediately effective. The first problem for an artist who wants to be successful is to learn how to use these elements—which isn't difficult to do, since they have to be simple or they lose their larger acceptance. The second problem for the artist is credibility—what he sings has to be believable. It has to become more than a manipulation of forms. The singer has to create an impression of being a symbol of the emotions that are at the center of the forms. Minnie began by using whatever forms she found around her, and she quickly found a way to express her own attitudes through them—or to create the impression this was what she was doing. In the popular arts this is good enough. At the height of her career she had found a clearly identifiable image which she was able to project as the center of her blues. Her career faltered when she couldn't project this image any longer and had to fall back on the forms around her, as she'd done twenty years before. The new styles and new attitudes didn't fit any longer, and what she was doing became obviously forced. This pattern can be superimposed over the career of any popular artist, white or black, since it is repeated over and over again with a relentless predictability. The surprise with Minnie is that she was able to continue it for so long, and she had one of the longest and most successful careers of any commercial blues artist of her time.

At the first session she and Joe did together she was overshadowed by his blues. Columbia brought them to New York and recorded six songs on June 18, 1929. The material was scheduled for release on their 14000 race series, and the first single was on sale on August 2. It was "That Will Be Alright" and "When the Levee Breaks," Col 14439, by "Kansas Joe and Memphis Minnie," though Joe sang both numbers. It sold as well as the other blues recordings Columbia was releasing at the time. The initial pressing order was 2950 copies, and there was an additional pressing of 3000 copies, a total of almost 6000 records. A Bessie Smith record issued two weeks earlier sold a little more than 8000 copies. "When the Levee Breaks" was one of Joe's finest recordings, a sensitive, emotional song that grew out of Mississippi floods of 1927—or out of other songs written about them—and their guitar accompaniment was a raggy duet finger-picked in the best Stokes and Sane style. They got confused in the first instrumental chorus following the vocal, when Minnie changed to the subdominant chord one beat too soon, but Joe changed to simple chording and held the rhythm until they got it together again for the next chorus. As a text the song was a clear example of what Joe could do as a blues writer—and what he couldn't do. The first verses were strong and direct, though their effect was weakened by standard lines like "Thinkin' about my baby and my happy home" and "I ain't got nobody to tell my troubles to." None of the details was strong enough to give the song a vividness that it lacked, though there was a clear overall mood. The thing that was most lacking was a definite self that dominated the song. The use of common verse material and the failure of the song to become more sharply visualized kept it from being a more successful blues text. These were habits that were to follow Joe through his career, and must have been among the reasons that his career lagged behind his wife's despite his early success.

If it keeps on rainin', levee's goin' to break
If it keeps on rainin', levee's goin' to break
And the water goin' come and we'll have no place to stay.

Well, all last night I sat on the levee and moaned
Well, all last night I sat on the levee and moaned
Thinkin' about my baby and my happy home.

It if keeps on rainin' levee's goin' to break
If it keeps on rainin' levee's goin' to break
And all these people will have no place to stay.

Now look here, mama, what am I to do
Now look here, mama, tell me what I can do
I ain't got nobody to tell my troubles to.

I works on the levee, mama, both night and day
I works on the levee, mama, both night and day
I ain't got nobody to keep the water away.

Oh cryin' won't help you, prayin' won't do no good
Oh cryin' won't help you, prayin' won't do no good
When the levee breaks, mama, you got to move.

I worked on the levee, mama, both night and day
I worked on the levee, mama, both night and day
So I worked so hard to keep the water away.

I had a woman, she wouldn't do for me
I had a woman, she wouldn't do for me
I'm goin' back to my used-to-be.

Oh, mean old levee caused me to weep and moan
It's a mean old levee caused me to weep and moan
Caused me to leave my baby and my happy home.

Columbia followed the first release with a second single several weeks later, on September 27. It was again two of Joe's vocals, "Goin' Back to Texas" and "Frisco Town," on Col 14455. They still had two titles, one of them Minnie's "Bumble Bee," but they held off on the release. Joe and Minnie had come back to Memphis, and they were there through the winter and spring of 1930, living just as they had been before the short New York trip. But Vocalion and Mayo Williams came into Memphis in February, and Mayo, with his usual commercial sense, realized that it was Minnie that should be recorded. In a series of sessions he recorded duets, with both of them singing and playing, and also songs of Minnie's, including her "Bumble Bee." The first thing he released from the sessions was "Bumble Bee" and "I'm Talking about You," on Vocalion 1476. "Bumble Bee" came out also on the other Vocalion labels—Banner, Oriole, Perfect, and Romeo. It was one of the year's most successful blues recordings, and it was one of Minnie's best known songs for several years. There were many copies of it and songs that used its imagery and its effect was wide-reaching. She recorded it again with the Memphis Jug Band on May 26 for Victor; then Columbia, realizing their mistake, put out their first version, with Joe's "I Want That" on the back of it, on August 15. But they'd waited too long, and it sold only 1100 copies, about the same sales they were getting on most of the country blues releases by this time. Minnie, by this point, had already moved to Chicago, and in July, a month earlier, she'd recorded "Bumble Bee No. 2" and a "New Bumble Bee." The song was a sexual blues, but it was fresher than most of them had been for some time, and there wasn't the heavy elaboration that dragged down the sexual blues the New York writers were turning out at the time. There was even a kind of innocence in her image of the bee as the male, the stinger as the penis, and the sting as the sexual embrace. In her different versions of it she usually described her bumble bee with a kind of loving admiration.

I got a bumble bee don't sting nobody but me
I got a bumble bee don't sting nobody but me
And I tell the world he got all the stinger I need.

And he makes better honey, any bumble bee I ever seen
And he makes better honey, any bumble bee I ever seen
And when he makes it, lord, how he makes me scream.

She even recognizes his casual amorality—"He get to flyin' and buzzin', stingin' everybody he meets"—but it doesn't anger her.

My bumble bee got ways just like a natural man
My bumble bee got ways just like a natural man
He stings somebody everywhere he lands.

As much as anything else it was the lack of even the pretense of anger that gave the song much of its freshness. As the blues was shifting closer to white popular song it was losing some of the desperate unhappiness that had characterized the infidelity theme in the twenties. Her lighter touch had a newer sound to it.

With 1930 came the beginning of America's slide into unemployment and chaos, and with this came a change in almost every aspect of American life. The twenties and everything they represented were swept away by the lines of unemployed on the streets, by the overloaded cars trying to get out of the South to jobs West or North—anywhere, by bank failures and drought, and a sudden realization that perhaps the United States hadn't found the answers to everything. The new seriousness of mood affected the blues, and it affected blues advertising. Almost overnight the caricature drawings on the advertisements disappeared, and the singers and performers who had been part of this period were swept away with them. The stereotype of the black entertainer at the beginning of the twenties was the blackface banjo player who told funny stories; by the end of the decade it was the chorus line of the musical *Shuffle Along*, Duke Ellington, and Louis Armstrong. The blues, at the edge of this tide, was dragged along with it. The most creative artists—who were still developing their blues out of their own experience—changed very little, but the newer popular blues artists, like Minnie, were to take the blues closer to popular music than it had come before.

Mayo Williams recognized Minnie's gift, and despite the financial crisis she was still selling records. He had her and Joe in the studio in Memphis in February; then, after Minnie had done the two sides with the Memphis Jug Band and some duets with her sister and her brother-in-law for Victor in May, she and Joe moved to Chicago and Mayo recorded them in June, July, August, and October. Minnie was just as active in the first few months of 1931—she did seventeen songs between January and May. With so much recording they had to use whatever kind of material they could find, and they did instrumental duets—like the Stokes-and-Sane-styled "Let's Go to Town" they recorded in March. Some of the songs were folk-like complex songs, similar to the kind of material the Memphis Jug Band was using—songs like "After While Blues," recorded in May. They did the old vaudeville blues "I Called You This Morning" as a duet, using the same melody that they'd used for the "Frisco Town" that Joe sang on their Columbia sessions in 1929. It was in this first period of her career that Minnie was successful simply because she was talented. She was working in the accepted styles, and she brought to them a clear, sincere voice, a great sense of song structure. There was also the same freshness to her imagery. She did songs with wonderfully light, expressive humor, like the talking story she did of a pet hog called Frankie Jean that wouldn't come unless it was whistled to. Williams released it as "Frankie Jean (That Trottin' Fool)" on Vocalion 1588 in the early fall of 1930.

Minnie and Joe were both fine guitarists, and their duets were interesting. Much of what they did came from their years of playing along Beale Street, but they'd also listened to recordings, and Minnie's single string melodic leads often sound like Lonnie Johnson. Both of them seem to be finger-picking; if they're using a flat pick they're very fast with it. The accompaniments were usually in first position chords, with a lot of string resonance and an emphasis on chord root tones that Joe played with his thumb. He played the second part, very strongly and fully, usually alternating a thumb bass note on the first and third beats of the measure and a strummed chord on the second and fourth—all of it set into a frame of runs and fills that doubled behind Minnie's more melodic leads. Most of this disappeared from her style when she learned barred chords and began using a flat pick a few years later, but at this period what she was doing was still close to the kind of music she'd been going when she was still called Kid Douglas and was living with Will Weldon not far from Beale Street.

In this period she still hadn't found the kind of self-projection that came later in her career, but she did one strong blues after another. She had the vividness of detail, the sense of personal identity in her songs that Joe didn't have. A song like "Crazy Cryin' Blues," with its high "crying" melismatic passages at the end of the lines, and its hummed choruses with an almost Mississippi-style intensity, shows clearly what she could do with the blues, and it shows how she was able to achieve much of her success. The verses are tightly interwoven, the musical setting is distinctive enough to set it apart as a song—the accompaniment is a wonderfully textured duet—and the sense of her place in the song, which she achieves by the careful use of details, gives the text something that Joe's "When the Levee Breaks" didn't have—the necessary feeling of personal identification, of an immediate personal credibility.

I been goin' crazy, I just can't help myself, uumh
I been goin' crazy, I just can't help myself, uumh
Because the man I'm lovin', he loves that someone else.

(The second verse is hummed as a kind of crying chorus.)

I was locked outdoors, sat on my steps all night long cryin', uumh
I was locked outdoors, sat on my steps all night long cryin', uumh
I was goin' crazy, crazy as I could be.

I got up this morning, I made a fire in my stove, uumh
I got up this morning, I made a fire in my stove, uumh
And made up my grain and stuck my pan outdoors.

I'm crazy, I'm crazy, just can't help myself, uumh
Crazy, I'm crazy, I just can't help myself, uumh
I'm as crazy , crazy, as a poor girl can be.

(The last verse is also a hummed cry.)

It was in the middle part of her career that Minnie was able to project a self-image that was broadly appealing to her audience. It was an image that was immediately recognizable—it was the same mistreated woman theme that had dominated the city blues of the twenties. In song after song she described herself in terms of rejection or betrayal by the men in her life.

> It's hard to be mistreated when you ain't done nothin' wrong
> It's hard to be mistreated when you ain't done nothin' wrong
> And it's hard to love a man when you can't keep him at home.

As she complained in one song, "Tell me, men, what do you expect us poor women to do?" Sometimes she tried to hold out for small favors:

> I'm so glad that I ain't nobody's fool
> I'm so glad that I ain't nobody's fool
> If I give you a dime of my money you sure got to come under my rule

but usually her mood was of simple resignation:

> It keeps me thinkin' and wonderin' all day time
> It keeps me thinkin' and wonderin' all day time
> Oh, people, it's so hard to please that man of mine. . . .

> Last night he started a argument
> He dared poor me to grunt
> Then taken my last dollar
> To get his girl friend drunk
> That keeps me thinkin', wonderin' all day time
> Oh, people, it's so hard to please that man of mine.

She was successful in projecting the sense of identity with her audience by her usual concern for small details that made the songs identifiable and by the sincerity of her own singing. Also the modesty of her accompaniments kept the feeling of shabby poverty that was the social context for what she sang. But it's also true that this was a self-image that she put on and off when she needed it. It's with performers like Minnie—as it was in the twenties with singers like Maggie Jones and Sara Martin—that the whole concept of the blues as a poetic, expressive art form breaks down. The blues she sang all through the thirties had little to do with the life she was living. She was a handsome, talented woman, with a successful career and an open enjoyment of the things of life she found around her. She made a comfortable living for the Depression years and she lived well in Chicago. Her marriage did end with Joe McCoy, but she didn't have the series of drab affairs that she described in her songs. The image which she projected of herself, however, was poor, often alone, often resentful—sometimes even pathetic in her need for affection.

> This same love dream come a tippin' through my room
> Same love dream come a tippin' through my room
> I got a letter from my dad say he'll be home soon.

It was this use of material that came from a common store of accepted attitudes that characterized the blues as popular music rather than folk expression. She lightened the image with a number of blues that expressed her pleasure with sexuality, and she responded to the lighter emotional mood of the thirties with a less tragic view of what was happening to her. She was resigned, but she could live through it. When she talks about an unfaithful lover in one of her more popular blues, she doesn't say that she's going to shoot him or throw herself in the river and drown. She simply shrugs and says, 'I'll hide my shoes somewhere near your shirttail." But her projection of this imagined self—this persona that she centered her blues around—was skillfully done. She was contintinually able to find verses with a newness and a freshness. It was her old skill with details and her sense of the verse image that somehow tied it together. In some of the blues the persona was so dominating that she even anticipated the situation and prepared for her lover to leave before he'd finally gone.

> Across the hill I built a lonesome shack
> Across the hill I built a lonesome shack
> So when my good man quit me I wouldn't have to beg him back.

She went on from this verse—which was almost self-defeating in its determination to avoid being defeated—to develop the other emotional suggestion in the verse—that she was going to find her way out of the situation with some degree of pride intact. She " . . . wouldn't have to beg him back."

> In the southeast corner that's where I put my cold iron bed
> In the southeast corner that's where I put my cold iron bed
> So when he put me out, have someplace to lay my head.

The whole determination to build some kind of place where she could get away does have a feeling of determination and pride to it, and the sudden detail "southeast corner" has a feeling of resourcefulness about it. She knows what she's doing.

> Buy my groceries and my stove where they are sellin' cheap
> Buy my groceries and my stove where they are sellin' cheap
> So when he starts beatin' me have some place to cook and eat.

The success of a blues text like this, of course, lies in its other levels of meaning. Most of the people who listened to her records were living, as she was, in cities; they certainly weren't going to build cabins anywhere, and most of them probably couldn't have pointed out a room's southeast corner in the slum tenements where they were living. But all of this was only an emotional metaphor for the deeper meaning, which was that a woman doesn't need to be helpless, that she can have her own strengths. Even if it's only a fantasy, she can retreat from the ugliness she can't get away from in her own life.

As a musician Minnie had changed considerably from the days when she had played along Beale Street. She learned to use barred chords, with their tighter, more choked sound, and she played a kind of suggested "swing" beat, a straight four chords to the measure with some emphasis on the off beat. It was much closer to the kind of rhythm that the popular black music had moved into, and it certainly helped her prolong her career. What she was playing was still danceable, even with the popularity of the new steps like the Lindy that came in in the mid-thirties. She did her first records without Joe in January 1935, and she recorded without a steady second guitarist until she married Ernest Lawlars, "Little Son Joe," and began recording with him in February 1939. In the four years that she was working alone she used a number of accompanists for her sessions. There were some brilliant piano from Black Bob, who did the instrumental solo on "Joe Louis Strut" in August 1935. Will Weldon— who was in Chicago now and beginning his successful career as Casey Bill— worked with her on steel guitar in October 1935 when she did four songs for Bluebird the same day he was in the studio. There's a second guitar on one of the songs he did, "Your Wagon's Worn Out Now," and it's probably Minnie.

For a brief period she experimented with small instrumental groups as accompaniment. The commercially oriented blues she was doing followed the trends in rhythm and accompaniments, even if the songs were left pretty much unchanged. Washboard Sam started recording not only with Big Bill on guitar and Black Bob on piano, but with an added clarinet, Arnett Nelson. The session was in June 1936. Five months later Minnie used a trumpet, along with Black Bob and a string bass player, for a session. At his next large group of sessions, in January 1937, Big Bill was using a trumpet also. It wasn't jazz, with the new instruments, but it wasn't as close to the blues as the simpler accompaniments had been. Even Casey Bill worked with a larger group for his sessions in the spring of 1937. The sophistication of the horns—despite the weakness of the trumpet player Minnie used—tended to work against the image that she, and the others, had been slowly building, and she stopped using heavier accompaniments after a session in December with Blind John Davis on piano, Arnett Nelson, clarinet, and a strong bass player. For her next sessions, in June 1938, she still had a piano and bass, but Charlie McCoy played mandolin. When she started recording in February 1939, she was with Little Son Joe, and they worked together for the next ten years.

There was a lot of recording during the entire period. The record industry was slowly pulling itself out of the worst of the Depression. It wasn't so much that there was more money anywhere—it was just that the companies, by price cutting, by placing records in corner variety stores, and by emphasizing more commercial material, had found new ways to get at what there was. If an artist, like Minnie, was selling, then they made sure there was always a new Memphis Minnie record for a customer to buy. Her Vocalion releases had been priced at 75 cents at the beginning of the thirties, but in 1935 they were selling for 35 cents, and everything she'd recorded for them was available. Between 1934 and the recording ban in 1942, there was a new Memphis Minnie record in the shops almost every month. Minnie wasn't getting rich from it—she was paid only $12.50 for every side she did—but there were some royalties from her compositions, and all the attention she was getting from the records kept her working steadily as long as she felt like playing. With this kind of pressure to turn out songs, all of the major artists of this period began to sound like each other as they went in and out of the studios with the same accompanists, and often the same kind of material, month after month. Minnie was the only woman with this kind of popularity, although Decca had Georgia White, who played the piano and had some of Minnie's success.

In 1941, after twelve years of recording, Minnie had another big success, like the "Bumble Bee" that had started everything off for her in 1929. She did a little song with a delayed verse form—a kind of sexual tease that suggested more than it actually said when she finished the verse. It was her "Me and My Chauffeur Blues," which she recorded on May 21, 1941. It was released with Can't Afford to Lose My Man" on OKeh 06288. She was still with the same record company, but the labels were being shifted, and her releases had been coming out on Okeh since the previous year. "Me and My Chauffeur" kept her career going for another ten years. It could have been the simplicity of the song that helped sell it, since it dealt with things like her not wanting her chauffeur to be riding those girls—which finished as riding those girls around—and was instantly memorable and earthily funny.

The melodies Minnie used for most of her blues in the 1934 to 1941 period, when she did much of her recording, were much simpler and less varied than the country song forms she and Joe had worked from in their first sessions. She still used the old "Sitting on Top of the World" melody—others turned up from time to time—but she'd stopped using the songs with repeated final refrains that she liked early in the thirties. Instead she was into a rather straight blues that was completely regular in its rhythm and harmonic changes. She used it over and over again, or with slight variations, for blues after blues. As always, with any artist who has recorded a great deal, there was considerably more variety in the texts than there was in the melodies.

In the south-east cor-ner, that's where I put my cold iron bed.

In the south-east cor-ner,— that's where I put my cold iron bed.

So when he put me out have some-place to lay my head.

With her warm, open voice, and the steady musicality of her guitar playing, she was able to bring a personal sense of identity to it. It was everybody's blues during these years, but Minnie could make you think, as long as you were listening to the record, that it was her blues, and she was still capable of recording songs that were as close to her own beginnings as songs she'd recorded back in Memphis with Kansas Joe.

I was born in Louisiana
I was raised in Algiers
And everywhere I been the peoples all say
"Ain't nothin' in ramblin', either in runnin' around"
Well I believe I'll marry, oh Lord, and settle down.

And occasionally she even allowed herself a larger comment on the social situation around her.

The peoples on the highway
Is walkin' and cryin'
Some is starvin', some is dyin'
Ain't nothin' in ramblin', either in runnin' around.
Well I believe I'll marry, oh Lord, and settle down.

In a large measure she deserved the success she had in her years living in Chicago.

She probably would have been able to pick up her career again after the blues revival began in the mid-fifties, but her husband, Ernest Lawlers, had a heart attack in 1957 and he had to stop playing. They went back to Memphis and she played occasionally around the city, but she wasn't well herself, and she didn't want to be away from him for long trips. She suffered a stroke in 1960; then he died a year later, leaving her in the care of her sister. She spent some time in a nursing home, in poverty and relative obscurity, even though there were friends in Memphis who were still in touch with her. Chris Strachwitz, of Arhoolie Records, reissued a number of her early recordings and was able to get royalties to her from the sales. The income helped her both financially and psychologically. When she suffered a third stroke she was moved from the nursing home back to her sister's house, and it was there that she died on August 7, 1972. She had outlived nearly all her contemporaries and, of all the musicians she had known and sang with along Beale Street, only Furry Lewis was there for the funeral. It was another reminder that the last days of the old Memphis blues styles had come after so many years of rich excitement and variety.

Atlanta

Atlanta.

10.
Atlanta

Sometimes, driving through the rolling hill land to get to Atlanta, it seems diffi-
cult to believe that the city will be there. There doesn't seem to be any reason
for one of the South's major metropolitan areas to be sprawled in this scrub
forest on the bank of the Chattahoochee River in north-central Georgia. The
Chattahoochee isn't a major river, the city isn't close to any important mineral
resources, and there's no feeling of the geography of the land leading you to
any kind of natural site. The trees on the rolling hills north of the city suddenly
thin out, the houses of the first suburbs begin to line themselves alongside the
highway; then the density of houses and cars thickens and you're in Atlanta. Of
all the cities in Georgia that could have been important, it would seem that
Savannah, on the Atlantic, and on the Savannah River, would have been the
state's dominant city, but Savannah is almost a backwater, hot and sticky and
a little crowded in the summers, quiet and a little out of the way in the winters.

Even with the relentless efficiency of modern highways and newer train sys-
tems, geography still holds some kind of sway over us, and Atlanta's position
perhaps reflects a little of this. It feels, as you come to Atlanta, as if you've
been hugging the edge of the Appalachian Mountains. If you want to go west
from the coastal states, the mountains push you away, and if you want to go
east from the southern countryside of Alabama or Mississippi, the lower lip of
the mountains holds you off. Atlanta is a kind of corner— a place where you
can turn. As you come down from the Carolinas on your way to New Orleans or
Jackson, Atlanta is the place where you swing from the eastern slope of the
mountains down to the southern hill country. If you're on a train coming east
from Birmingham on your way to Richmond you'll be routed through Atlanta
to get under the mountains. The mountains are more easily crossed now—the
roads are better and the train systems service the whole mountain area—but At-
lanta was built in an earlier period, and it has kept its position and grown and
stretched itself into the South's most modern and prosperous city.

Atlanta, in its central city, isn't much larger than Memphis. Each of them has about half a million people. Atlanta, however, is the center of a large suburban area, and its total population is closer to a million. Outside of Memphis, you're into the red earth/timber/farm country before you've gone too far. Around Atlanta you're still in the suburbs. Also, Atlanta's period of growth came later; so it's a more modern city. But as musical centers, both of them were small, and there was no center of recording or musical activity for either of them. Each of them had a theater that was important to the black community—the Palace on Beale Street and the Bailey Theatre on Decatur Street, the center of Atlanta's black neighborhood. The theaters brought them into contact with the touring reviews and stage shows, as well as using local talent for occasional presentation, but the recording companies came through only on an irregular basis. The musicians themselves, in both cities, came in from the surrounding countryside. Memphis had the Mississippi Delta to draw upon for its bluesmen, so there was a clearer definition of sources for much of the music recorded in Memphis. Atlanta, in contrast, seemed to be centered in an area without a dominant rural style; so the blues recorded there seems only fitfully to glimpse back to an earlier songster or work song tradition.

This doesn't mean that Decatur Street, sloping down into the lowland off Peachtree Street, with its line of shabby storefronts and barbershops, had no local blues style. The Atlanta singers were distinctive in everything they did, from the way they played the guitar to the way they conceived blues rhythms to they way they sang, but it seems to be a tradition developed more in the back streets in Atlanta and influenced by the phonograph record in a way the Memphis tradition was not. This seems to be most clearly reflected in the rhythmic pulse, which in the blues of other areas is closely related either to a songster tradition or to the work and gang songs. The Atlanta musicians often used a kind of strumming that had no clearly defined rhythmic character. The older ones, like Peg Leg Howell, were closer to a folk orientation, and some of Howell's best blues were half-remembered songs from the earlier period, and he used a number of finger-picking styles, as well as the strumming beat. Also his recordings with his "Gang," a loose street group in the eastern skiffle tradition, had some of the rough exuberance of the country dance. It's in the singing of the younger men, such as Barbecue Bob (Robert Hicks), that the lack of a strong relationship to a larger area style is seen most. This didn't affect his popularity in any way, and he was one of the most successful bluesmen of the period, but it does seem to hem in his creativity at moments. The Atlanta style is a fascinating hybrid of irregular chantlike rhythms and uniquely personal harmonic and structural forms. It is perhaps best typified by Robert Hicks, but other singers, less well known, such as Willie Baker and Curley Weaver, could sing in the style with considerable effectiveness, and their "Atlanta-styled" numbers, such as Baker's "Weak Minded Blues" or Weaver's "No No Blues"—probably learned from Hicks—are distinctively part of the blues along Decatur Street.

There also seemed to be a predilection for the twelve-string guitar in Atlanta, which also is unusual in rural blues since it's very difficult to choke the third string for the kind of modal tonalities that are common in blues from other areas. The harmonic forms are generally derived from the urban twelve-bar form, though often there is a distinct pause at the vocal phrase ending, emphasizing the harmonic change, and often there are unrelated tones included in the chord grouping. The vocal tone is generally very strong and somewhat low in pitch, the sound coming from the back of the mouth with the throat rather tight. It isn't one of the prettiest vocal sounds in the blues, but it has a harsh effectiveness against the twanging tone of the twelve-string. The vocal scale has many elements of the urban blues scale—that is, with a conscious use of the flatted third and the flatted seventh tones—but often the voice treats the third as a more neutral tone, with its modality more ambiguous. The mode is closer to the white scale of much Southern singing and may reflect a closer musical relationship between the races at the point when the vocal style was forming. This tonal ambiguity, set against the irregular phrase rhythm of the voice, and the hard, rough vocal tone contrasting with the doubled jangling of the guitar's upper strings are the dominant elements of the Atlanta style, and for a brief period, because of Hick's popularity, the style became rather widely known.

It was such a unique style, however, and so closely identified with a local area, that it didn't have a long life, and it has almost completely been lost, even in Atlanta itself. Some of the vocal intonation is still there in Atlanta singing, and sometimes there's some of the old twanging strum, but it's the Piedmont guitar style that's dominant throughout the area—or at least dominant to the extent that traditional blues survive at all in Atlanta. It's now a modern city, rushing into the new American future, and it doesn't seem to be a future that includes the older blues.

As in Memphis, the character of the recording done in Atlanta reflects the personality of the recording director who was most responsible for that recording. In Memphis it was Ralph Peer; and in Atlanta it was Columbia's recording director, Frank Walker, who most shaped the picture we have of Atlanta's music. Walker was interviewed by Mike Seeger in 1962, and, although he didn't have detailed recollections of the recordings he did there, his answers suggested some of the attitudes he brought to his sessions. Walker, unlike Peer, was born in the country, on a farm in Fly Summit, New York, and his father died when he was six, forcing the widow to put him with another family. He worked as a farmhand until he was eighteen; then he went into Albany to a business college to learn shorthand stenography and later worked as a secretary to the president of a local bank. He worked other jobs, moved to New York City, then was in the Navy from 1916 to February 1919. He found himself in the record business a few months later, mostly by accident. As he told Seeger:

> Well, it so happened when you got out of the service in those days there was very little happening in the line of work. My concern was liquidated. There were no jobs available. Soldiers and sailors were selling apples on the streets of New York and all over the country. There were no such things as jobs. I had offered my services for as low as fifteen dollars a week. I couldn't find a job.

So finally one day I happened to run into a man on the street whose name was Frances S. Whiten. He was a Commander in the Navy, a position above mine, and I had done something that he had admired very much that had gotten him written up in the Congressional Record. He asked where I was working and I said, "I wish I were."

"Well," he said, "I am a nephew of the Duponts and we own Columbia Phonograph and Dictaphone Corporation and you're coming over and work for me." I said, "I don't know anything about a phonograph record," and he said, "Neither do I, so you can be my assistant."

He trained in Columbia's Bridgeport factory, then left Columbia for a brief period to run a concert management agency in Detroit. In 1921 he was back at Columbia and ready to begin his work as an artist and repertory director. As he told Seeger, he first went into the South with portable equipment in the twenties largely because of his "first love" for country music. Columbia began their 15000 white folk music series to accommodate the material he was bringing back with him. At the same time, as he didn't tell Seeger, he had become one of the most important figures in the blues recording industry, and artists he worked with included Bessie Smith, most of the other major urban blues artists of the period, and jazz artists ranging from King Oliver to the New Orleans Owls. Clarence Williams, who was an assistant of Walker's during some of this period, recalled that he had almost complete freedom in his choice of artists and recording. The Columbia race series, the famed 14000 series, began in November 1923—first it was a 13000 series but, after eight releases, worry over the implications of the number 13 induced Columbia to change the numbering. For the next ten years Walker was recording for both series, the country and the race series, on regular trips through the South.

. . . As business grew, we made periodical trips to the South and at least two trips a year. We had a rather bad time of it if we recorded less than two hundred masters on each trip. Now, not all of these found the market. It's not like today, with the taping and so forth. In those days the recording was done on solid wax and you had to bring containers of the waxes you used. So you were very careful and choosy. . . .

Walker sent word ahead to local distributors or retailers who were working with him as scouts, and they got out word to any musicians in the area that Columbia's unit would be in town to record. Walker himself made all decisions on both artists and their repertoire, unlike Paramount, which often let their scouts send the artists on to Chicago, where the decisions were made. He worked, roughly, on an alternating weekly basis, recording country artists one week, then black artists the next, though sometimes the two necessarily overlapped. About Atlanta he remembered, in his interview with Seeger:

We recorded in a little hotel in Atlanta, and we used to put the singers up and pay a dollar a day for their food and a place to sleep in another little old hotel. And then we would spend all night going from one room to another, and they kept the place hopping all night in all the different rooms that they were in. You would have to go from one room to another and keep your pen working and decide we won't use this and pick out the different songs that they knew, because you couldn't bring songs to them because they couldn't learn them. Their repertoire would consist of eight or ten things that they did well, and that was all they knew.

So, when you picked out the three or four that were best in a man's so-called repertoire you were through with that man as an artist. It was all. It was a culling job, taking the best that they had. You might come out with two selections or you might come out with six or eight, but you did it at that time. You said goodbye. They went back home. They had made a phonograph record, and that was the next thing to being President of the United States in their mind.

Then, out of it, there were a very few who could learn or could adopt something that somebody else might be able to do but not record. So you might put those two together, so that one might be able to teach the other and you came up with a saleable or recordable product. . . .

Walker came to Atlanta to record his country artists, such as Riley Pickett and Gid Tanner and the Skillet Lickers. These were the names he remembered from the artists he worked with there, and the things he'd recorded that he remembered best were the raw country vaudeville sketches like "Corn Likker Still in Georgia" that he wrote for them with a man working at the Atlanta radio station, Dan Hornsby. They were broad, obvious, rural humor, and they sold, as Walker remembered, ". . . in the hundreds of thousands." Nothing he did with his blues artists was as successful, even though the artists he recorded included Peg Leg Howell, Barbecue Bob, Charley Lincoln, and Blind Willie McTell. The Atlanta blues that we have on record are—to a large degree—the material he decided to record on those long nights before the sessions when he tried to "cull" what would sell best. Perhaps this, as much as any other factor, has shaped the musical picture that emerges of the Atlanta bluesmen.

11.
Peg Leg Howell

Of all the voices from Atlanta in the twenties, the one that seems to come out of the oldest tradition—the one that seems most closely tied to a half-forgotten, quietly introspective music from the farm cabins and the still crossroads—is Peg Leg Howell. He was the the first country bluesman to be recorded for Columbia's race catalog, and there was something in his music that was deeply entwined with the Georgia countryside, with its soft sunlight and hazy sky and lingering summers. In the fifties on trips to Atlanta, it didn't seem possible that he could still be living, and questioning people along Decatur Street was sourly discouraging. But people in a hard, poor neighborhood can be silent with a stranger, until they have some idea what he's asking about. A man would stop and think a minute. "Yes, I 'member that old man, but he hasn't been 'round here for a long time." But by the sixties the interest in the older blues had spread even to Atlanta. Three young enthusiasts, George Mitchell, Roger Brown, and Jack Boozer, stopped in one of the noisy, crowded barbershops on Decatur Street where the response in 1958 had been only guarded stares. As Mitchell wrote later, in the notes to an album of Howell's blues:

> When we stopped at Shorters' Barber Shop, one of the oldest establishments on Decatur Street, we decided to ask about additional blues singers as well. After mentioning Peg Leg Howell, ten men gathered around us offering to lead us to him.

> Finally after the confusion had subsided and we had gotten over our shock, we picked two of the men to take us to Howell. We rode about a mile past Capitol Square, turned into a dirt road and pulled up in front of Howell's small and shabby house. Our guides were knocking loudly on the door when we heard the faint voice of a very old man telling us to come in. The house was dark and musty, but the moment I saw Howell sitting in his wheelchair in the back room,

103

I recognized him from his pictures. He appeard to be very old, was unshaven, and had no legs. Just seconds after I introduced myself, he eagerly reached for the guitar I was holding. He took it in his large, worn hands and immediately began singing and playing. He sang in a deep, moaning, almost inaudible voice, but we could still make out the words:

Some folks say them worried blues ain't bad,
Yes, some folks say them worried blues ain't bad,
But they's the worst old feeling that ever I had. . . .

Peg Leg—his real name was Joshua Barnes Howell—was seventy-five when he was found again in Atlanta, and the years of lonely poverty had left their mark. After a month of practicing with the guitar he recorded again in an Atlanta studio, but the music was only fitfully reminiscent of what he had created thirty-five years before. Of greater importance was the opportunity to learn more from him about the early period of Georgia music. As he told Mitchell:

. . . I was born on the fifth of March in 1888. I was born in Eatonton, Putnam County, Georgia. I am 75 years old.

My father was a farmer. When I was a child I went to school in Putnam County; I went as far as the ninth grade before I stopped. After that I worked on my father's farm with him . . . plowed. Worked on the farm until 1916, when I was about 28.

Then I worked at a fertilizer plant in Madison, Ga., on the Georgia Road to Augusta. I had lost my leg in 1916 and had to quit farm work. I got shot by my brother-in-law; he got mad at me and shot me. That's how I lost my leg. I worked at the fertilizer plant for a year. After that I didn't do much, just messed around town. I came to Atlanta when I was about 35 years old. I just got tired of staying in a small town. I didn't do much of anything in Atlanta when I came there either.

I learned how to play the guitar about 1909. I learnt myself—didn't take long to learn. I just stayed up one night and learnt myself.

The men from Columbia records found me there in Atlanta. A Mr. Brown—he worked for Columbia—he asked me to make a record for them. I was out serenading, playing on Decatur Street and he heard me playing out on the street. This was around 1927, I think, but it could have been earlier.

Peg Leg Howell (right) and his gang, with Eddie Anthony playing violin.

It was probably Frank Walker who supervised Peg's first session, on November 8, 1926, during one of his visits to Atlanta to record country artists. He'd been recording black artists in Atlanta, but they had been gospel groups or the popular preachers, like Rev. J.M. Gates, who had recorded for him earlier in the year. Peg did four songs for the first sessions, "Coal Man Blues," "Tishamingo Blues," "New Prison Blues," and "Fo' Day Blues." The last two songs were released first, on Columbia 14177-D. The day of release was the 30th of December 1926, and the record was listed in the February 1927 advertising supplement. It was relatively successful for the period, with an initial pressing of 5250 copies and a second pressing of 4000 copies, but the sales didn't compare with either the best of the gospel groups or the established blues artists. A record by the Birmingham Jubilee Singers released the same day sold 16, 725 copies, and a Bessie Smith record issued two weeks later sold 23,700.

For the next two and a half years Walker continued to record Howell, but his career, like his songs, was modest. Walker decided to record him with a group, and for the next two sessions, in April and November of 1927, he recorded him with his friends Eddie Anthony, who played violin, and Henry Williams, who played guitar. The first of their releases by Peg Leg Howell and His Gang, "Jelly Roll Blues" and "Beaver Slide Rag"—which went on sale on May 30, 1927, on Columbia 14210-D—was his most successful record, and it sold a total of 12,950 copies. It was a fresh, raucous country stomp, played with noisy enthusiasm, and it deserved to be successful. Peg's own songs were softer, more subtle, often tracing motifs and scenes from a country life that was almost forgotten by the new audience in the cities. He recorded by himself again on November 9, 1927, and he did his beautiful "Skin Game Blues," with its evocation of the work camps and their endless, fierce card games. There was another solo session the next spring, on April 20, 1928, where he did four songs, but the rest of his recording was with other instrumentalists. Eddie Anthony sang and played with him the next October; there was an unknown violinist for his session on April 10, 1929; then he and a friend named Jim Hill did four last songs three days later. These records were released over the next eighteen months, but there was no further work for Peg. He hadn't made much money from his music, but they'd paid him $50 for the first record, and there had been steady advances and royalties, and he had some chances to sing in the bars when the records were coming out. When his recording career was over he was forty-one, and he drifted back to the life he'd been leading before Columbia heard him on the street.

Where did Howell's songs come from? He had a much wider range of song than other Atlanta artists, and his guitar playing, despite its limitations, used a number of techniques, from complex finger-picking, to more standard picked blues, to exciting work with open tunings and a metal finger slide. On his recordings he sounded like a quiet, introspective performer, and certainly he had almost none of the sexual assertiveness of other bluesmen of the period. There is little specific erotic content in any of his songs. He could even be awkwardly self-pitying, in songs like "Rocks and Gravel" or "Please Ma'am." "Please Ma'am" has a kind of desperate hopelessness to it.

Please ma'am, please ma'am please,
Take me back, try me one more time,
Please ma'am, please ma'am, please,
Don't you want no more to take me back,
Please ma'am.

Been begging you all night long,
I'll acknowledge I've done wrong,
Please ma'am, please, take me back,
Try me one more time, please ma'am

Begging you all night long,
I'll acknowledge I've done wrong,
Please ma'am, take me back,
Try me one more time,
Won't do wrong no more, please ma'am,
Please take me back,
Try me one more time,
Please ma'am. . . .

Some of his songs seem to suggest that he came out of a tradition that was losing ground in the country areas even when he was young, and some of what he recorded has no clear antecedent in either of the area's cultures. He says that he wrote some of the material he recorded, and, since he clearly remembers the source for many of his songs, his claim to have written others has to be taken seriously, even though all of his songs have considerable cultural reference. Like many other country artists of the late twenties he was influenced by other recordings, and there is considerable eclecticism in his blues pieces, just as there was in the work of the other Atlanta musicians. Songs like "Low Down Rounder's Blues" and "Doin' Wrong" use melodic lines and guitar patterns influenced by Blind Lemon Jefferson; on other songs, among them "Broke and Hungry Blues," he tries to imitate Lonnie Johnson's distinctive guitar style. He'd been singing on the streets with a mandolin player—Eugene Pedin, who never recorded—when Columbia first heard him, and he seemed to work well with other musicians, so Frank Walker was justified in using Eddie Anthony to work with him on many of the pieces he did. There was a photo of Peg in the 1927 Columbia catalog that reflected the mood of his music. He was portly, half smiling, with a careful moustache, and—for some reason—a white skull cap. He was wearing a white shirt and tie, a striped sweater, and a dark suit jacket. The text was the usual string of clichés.

When "Peg Leg" Howell lost his leg, the world gained a great singer of blues. The loss of a leg never bothered "Peg Leg" as far as chasing around after blues is concerned. He sure catches them and then stomps all over them.

Nobody ever knows just what will happen when "Peg Leg" Howell is let loose with a guitar, but it always is sure to be good.

When he talked about his music in 1963 he confirmed that much of what he'd learned came from the country and that much of the music outside of the city was sung without accompaniment. This would seem to explain the problem some of the Atlanta singers had of relating the vocal melody to their guitar style. "I learned many of my songs around the country. I picked them up from anybody—no special person. Mostly they just sang, didn't play anything." Other songs that he did were derived from his own experience. He heard the "New Prison Blues," his first release, when he was in prison himself. "In 1925 I had been in prison for selling whiskey and I hear the song there. I don't know who made it up. As for selling the whiskey, I would sell it to anybody who came to the house. I bought the moonshine from people that ran it and I sold it. I don't know how they caught me; they just ran down on me one day." The "Jelly Roll Blues" came from a man named Elijah Lawrence, who was singing it in the country.

Of all the songs he recorded, however, some of the best were things that he wrote himself. "Some of the songs I made up. 'Too Tight' was one; 'Rocks and Gravel' was another. That's really about the blues, that 'Rocks and Gravel'. Just made 'em up and played 'em. 'Coal Man Blues'—I wrote that too. 'Skin Game Blues'—that's about gambling. Skin game is a card game."

"Rocks and Gravel" was one of his less interesting pieces, but the last two songs he mentioned are perhaps his most interesting. They seem drawn from a large cultural area, and they have elements of urban white material as well as rural black. "Coal Man Blues" is sung to a complex finger-picked accompaniment, the guitar following the voice over and over in its hurried sixteen-measure verses. The harmony is unusual; what is outlined in the finger-picking is a repeated patter of I - IV - I - IV, I - I - V - I. The song has ballad elements, coal vendors' street cries, and blues verses, all of them somehow merging into the song's overall dimensions. It begins with a sharp image of city life, seemingly outside of the kind of experience that was part of Howell's own life.

> Woke up this mornin' 'bout 5 o'clock,
> Got me some eggs and a nice po'k chop,
> Cheap cigar and a magazine,
> Had to run pretty fast to catch the 5:15.

The next verse is related to it, but it has some of the character of a street ballad, half remembered in its details.

> Let me tell you something that I seen
> Coal man got run over by the 5:15
> Cut off his arms and it crushed his ribs.
> Did the poor man die? No, the poor man lives.

This is followed by another verse about the accident, giving a different train number and making it clear that the coal man is dead. The fourth verse is a street vendor's cry.

Hard coal, stovewood man,
Hard coal and the stovewood man,
I ain't got but a little bit left,
If you don't come get it gonna burn it myself.

There are more street vendor cries, then the song shifts again and begins to take on a blues tinge.

Sell it to the rich and I sell it to the poor
Sell it to the rich and I sell it to the poor
Sell it to the rich and I sell it to the poor
Sell it to the nice brown that's standin' at the door.

Furnish your wood, furnish your coal
Furnish your wood and I furnish your coal
Furnish your wood and I furnish your coal,
Make you love me doggone your soul.

By the end it has become a blues, still repeating over and over its breathless melody.

Let me tell you, mama, what's the matter now
Let me tell you, mama, what's the matter now
Let me tell you, mama, what's the matter now
You don't want me, take me anyhow.

The verses seem to come from such diverse sources that much of the song is clearly not original, but he has put it together with a naive excitement, and with the distinctiveness of the finger-picking it is a remarkable performance.

"Skin Game Blues" is a unique masterpiece, and in it all the things in his style that were most individual contributed to the effectiveness of the performance. The guitar is in an open tuning, and he plays the same kind of running rhythm that he used on "Please Ma'am." He uses a slide on the upper strings and the guitar plays a unison melody with the voice. The verses are richly textured in a complex structure that uses spoken interjections, a balladlike refrain, and a series of references to other gambling songs sung everywhere in the rural United States. In its overall form a verse melody is used at the larger division points in the song, and it is followed with a subsidiary verse melody that is sometimes used without the opening verse, and there is a refrain that alternates with them.

I (Guitar tuned open; accompaniment picked on chord tones.)

When I came to Geor-gie mon-ey and clothes I

had, babe, All the mon-ey I had done gone, my Sun-day clothes in pawn, Sun-day clothes in pawn, Sun-day clothes in pawn, lo-vin' babe, my Sun-day clothes in pawn.

After the spoken interjection "Hold the cards, dollar more, two more a half," recited in rhythm with the guitar, the singing returns with the same melody as "Sunday clothes in pawn."

Dollar more, the deuce beat a nine,
Dollar more, the deuce beat a nine, lovin' babe,
Dollar more, the deuce beat a nine.

When I (did?) the skin game last night, thought I'd have some fun,
Lost all the money that I had, babe,
Had to pawn my special gun.

Had to pawn my special gun,
Had to pawn my special gun, lovin' baby,
Had to pawn my special gun.

(refrain)
Say, you better let a deal go down, skin game comin' to a close,
And you better let the deal go down.

Well, gambled all over Missouri, gambled all through Spain, babe,
Police come to arrest me, babe, and they did not know my name.

And they did not know my name,
And they did not know my name, lovin' baby,
And they did not know my name.

(refrain)
Better let a deal go down, skin game comin' to a close,
And you better let the deal go down.

Spoken:
    Hold the cards, dollar more, deuce beat a nine,
    Add more, two, put up over there, nigger.

(refrain)
    Better let the deal go down,
    Said you better let the deal go down.

    Gambled all over Missouri, gambled through Tennessee, babe,
    Soon as I reached ol' Georgie, the niggers carried a handcuff to me.

    The niggers carried a handcuff to me, babe,
    The niggers carried a handcuff to me, lovin' baby,
    And the niggers carried a handcuff to me.

(refrain)
    Better let a deal go down, skin game comin' to a close,
    And you better let the deal go down.

The last verse is difficult to interpret since during this period no black man in the South was performing a police function, but within the context of the song it seems to have an emotional extension from the first reference to "Georgie" in the opening verse. It was not the kind of song that was selling to blues audiences, and, although the record had an initial pressing of 2310 copies and a second of 2000, it is difficult to believe that it was in any way possible for a recording like this to be made in a commercial context. It's performances like "Skin Game Blues" that give the early country blues its importance in the history not only of American song but also of American folk culture.

The recordings ended for Peg in 1929, and a few years later he stopped playing completely. His friend Eddie Anthony died in 1934, and he didn't want to play without him. "After my last record, I just stopped recording. Didn't make no more. After I stopped recording, I just played around town. I went back to selling liquor. Then I ran a woodyard for about two years around 1940. I lost my other leg in 1952. Through sugar diabetes.

"Through the years I have lived all over the city, moved all over. I haven't done much playing over the years until recently. After Eddie Anthony died, I just didn't feel like playing any more. . . ." There was no more recording after the album that George Mitchell did in 1963, and except for some reissues of his older songs Peg is still a lesser known figure in the blues. But he occupies a significant niche in the development of the Atlanta blues, and in his finest songs he was able to add a small, but personal, dimension to the blues itself.

12.
The Hicks Brothers—
Barbecue Bob and
Laughing Charley

"What you laughin' at, Charley?"
"Well, I done laughin' at you how you tryin' to barbecue that meat."
"I don't see anythin' funny about that."
"Ain't you 'fraid you'll get burnt?"
"Oh no, I know my stuff on that, I'm makin' it good and juicy. That way the people like it, you know, these days, with the gravy runnin' out."

Barbecue Bob and Laughing Charley,
Atlanta, November 9, 1927.

The music of the Hicks brothers is remarkable for its lack of roots in a local blues tradition. They were among the early country singers to be extensively recorded, and over a period of three and a half years there was a great deal of recording, particularly of Bob. If there were a strongly identifiable blues style from rural Georgia it would have been evident in the material they recorded, but the sense is more of a broad eclecticism than of a clearly defined response to the life in the small farm towns they grew up in. What they shared with the other Atlanta singers was a sound in their voice, a halting, inner centering of the vocal rhythm, and the sweeping ring of their guitar playing. But even if their music doesn't have an immediate textual identity, or a feeling of a shared body of song material that they drew from—as the Memphis musicians had with their medicine shows—there is a sad, lingering, haunting plaintiveness in what they sang, and it transcended the occasional dated humor and the stiff imitativeness of some of Bob's recordings. If there is any one thing that characterizes their music it's their sometimes embarrassed, sometimes clumsy, but deep and obvious sincerity. Whatever the response was to the music of the Hicks brothers, it was music that stayed in the ear, and even if it was overshadowed by the greater brilliance and musical depth of singers from other parts of the South, their music wasn't forgotten.

Like the other Atlanta musicians, they came in from the country. They grew up on a farm in Walton County, about twenty-five miles east of Atlanta. The country is flattening as the land drops away from the last hump of the Appalachians, and east of Atlanta it's rolling country, with brush in the stream beds and a deep, loamy quality to the earth. The soil is still red-brown, but there isn't so much of the raw erosion that has gouged out the hill country to the northwest. There's a greenness to the land all year round; even when the leaves fall from the hardwoods the grass is still thick and green, and there are sprays of leaves on the spiny brush. The farms have spread over the best of the land, and the fields have been deep plowed to get the last bit of richness out of the soil. When the Hicks boys were growing up it was still cotton country, though there weren't the oppressive flat miles of dusty fields as in the Mississippi Delta. But even though the farms were smaller they were just as poor, and it was the same relentless yearly circle of planting, weeding, picking in the long months of spring and summer.

Charley was the older brother, born about 1899. Bob was two and half years younger, born in 1902. And they were close, as brothers—there's a warmth between them on their recordings together, a feeling of things lived through together. Charley started playing first, and Bob picked it up from him when he was fourteen. A sister still lives in Atlanta, where she was interviewed by George Mitchell, and she felt that Bob was the better guitar player, but Charley had a better voice. Their closeness is evident on their first recording together, "It Won't Be Long Now, Parts 1 and 2," Columbia 14268-D. After their self-conscious dialog about Bob's job in the barbecue shack and their troubles with their girls, they sing a blues together, and the style they sing in is Charley's—a difficult, irregularly structured blues, with a complicated vocal melody. They sing and play in unison, something almost unheard of in blues duets, but Bob's affection for his older brother would seem to have extended to his brother's music, and he could remember what he'd learned well enough to match the guitar playing and the vocal inflection almost exactly, in a rumbling, steamy, dark sound.

Charley had earned the money for his guitar by picking cotton, and both of them were used to hard work. Their sister said that they came into Atlanta about 1920. Bob was just eighteen. He worked as a yardman for a time, then when the Biltmore Hotel was completed he went to work there, and from the hotel he started working as a carhop at a barbecue shack in Buckhead, a rich white neighborhood in Atlanta. When it wasn't too busy he played for the customers while they ate and they took him out to play for parties when the barbecue shack closed for the night. He got his nickname from the job. He started there about 1925, and he'd been there two years when Columbia records heard of him and sent a man out to find him. The companies had only been recording country blues for a little more than a year when he went into the studio, and in Atlanta there'd been very little earlier recording. Peg Leg Howell had done four songs for Columbia the November before, and there'd been enough interest for Columbia to try to find new artists in the area.

Bob was the first of the brothers to record. He did "Barbecue Blues" and "Cloudy Sky Blues" on Friday, March 25, 1927, during a two-week period of recording that Frank Walker supervised in Atlanta. All the recording was done in a downtown hotel and there were more than two hundred songs recorded, all but thirty of them by Columbia's white artists. Bob's recording was released on May 10 on Columbia 14205D, with an initial pressing of 10,850 copies. In this first enthusiam over the country blues the new recordings sold very well; it was still a new style of blues—as far as the people buying records were concerned—and there weren't that many recordings. The record was advertised in the June catalog supplement, and there was an additional pressing of 5000 records. This was a total sale of nearly 16,000 copies of a first record of a new artist who was completely unknown outside of Atlanta. A fine Bessie Smith record issued a month later, "Send Me to the 'Lectric Chair," sold a thousand copies less. Walker was pleased enough to bring Bob to New York a month after the record was released to record again. Bob's sister says that he went to New York by train with a manager and that they wrote the first song he recorded there, "Mississippi Heavy Water Blues," on the train on the way up. It was one of the many songs about the Mississippi River floods of the winter before, and it was probably his best known recording, though its sales weren't exceptionally high. Copies of the record—on Columbia 14222D, with "Mama You Don't Suit Me" on the other side—turned up for years in junk shops and Salvation Army stores everywhere in the South, and almost all of them were gray and worn with endless playing.

Bob stayed with the well-known OKeh artist Mamie Smith, who had a large house in Harlem, and he did two sessions in New York. On the first, June 15, 1927, he did the "Mississippi Heavy Water Blues" and "Mama You Don't Suit Me " and two other blues, "Brown-Skin Gal" and "Honey You Don't Know My Mind." The next day he did four more songs, but since Walker was always looking for other kinds of songs he thought he could sell, two of the songs were gospel pieces. Bob did the blues "Poor Boy a Long Ways from Home " and "Easy Rider, Don't You Deny My Name " and the gospel songs "When the Saints Go Marching In" and "Jesus' Blood Can Make Me Whole." The religious pieces were his next Columbia release, on August 20. To keep the two styles of music separate Columbia used his own name, Robert Hicks, for the religious recording, while the blues releases were always by Barbecue Bob. The two religious songs sold almost as well as the blues pieces—there was an initial pressing of 6775 copies and a second pressing of 4000—but he was a blues singer, not a guitar evangelist, and he didn't record religious material again.

For most of the bluesmen who went north to record, the cities were too difficult to deal with, and when they'd finished with the work in the studio they went back to the South. Bob was back in Atlanta for the rest of the summer, and he recorded for three days when Walker and the Columbia engineers were in town in November. Charley also started his recording career at the same group of sessions. He did six blues on November 4, the next day Bob did four songs, on the ninth they did their duet, and the next day Bob did two final blues. Probably it was Bob who got his brother the studio sessions, since the companies always asked their artists if there was anybody else they knew about who could come in and sing. Peg Leg Howell was recorded during the same group of sessions, along with the popular Columbia white artists who were centered in Atlanta.

The duet "It Won't Be Long Now" was the first release from everything that they'd recorded. Frank Walker rushed it into the stores, and it was released only a few weeks after they'd sung it, on December 20, 1927. Whether it was the season, or the song, or just the new sound of their Atlanta music, the record was a big success. With two pressings it sold 16,750 copies, more than any other release on the race series in this period. To follow up on its success Charley's first recording was released only three weeks later, on January 10, and a new record of Bob's came out on January 30. Charley's—under the name Laughing Charley, because of the laugh he used to start some of his songs—was his "Hard Luck Blues" and "Chain Gang Trouble" on Columbia 14272D. At first his records sold as well as Bob's. The two releases in January each sold about 12,000 copies, Bob's 11,295 and Charley's 11,600. They each had a record out in April, but this time Bob's sold 14,425 and Charley's only 9300. Charley's record was later to be one of his better known ones, "Jealous Hearted Blues" and "My Wife Drove Me from the Door," because copies continually turned up when collectors went through the South digging out the old blues recordings, and most of the copies were virtually unplayed.

In the next trip to Atlanta, in April 1928, the same month they each had a record out, Walker recorded both of the brothers again, Charley on April 11— he did four songs—and Bob on April 13 and 21—he did eight songs in the two sessions. Only two of Charley's were released, one with the startling title "If It Looks Like Jelly, Shakes Like Jelly, It Must Be Gelatine," which sold poorly, only 6350 copies. He was recorded only twice again as a solo performer—once the next fall and in the spring of 1930. They did another duet together at the same time, a minstrel show recording of "coon" material, "Darktown Gamblin'—the Crap Game" and "Darktown Gamblin'—the Skin Game." It was released under their own names, Robert and Charley Hicks. It had some similarities to the kind of skits Walker had been successful with using his "hillbilly" artists, but it came too late to sell to the vanishing blues audience in 1930.

Bob had gone on to become an established artist and he was recorded every time Columbia was in Atlanta. Over the three and a half years he was a Columbia artist he did sixty titles, and his releases sold almost 200,000 copies—198,365 were pressed and usually all copies were shipped to stores during this period. He consistently outsold every artist on the Columbia race series except Bessie Smith, Ethel Waters, and Blind Willie Johnson for the years he was recording. It's difficult to tell what he might have earned in royalties from his recordings. There are no composer credits on any of his songs, which usually meant that the performer was paid a flat fee for the copyright. Record royalties were sometimes a flat fee, but usually for someone like Bob there was a regular royalty paid, often 1½ cents a side. This would have given him an income of almost $6,000 if he was being paid this royalty. Certainly his sister remembers it as a time when her brother lived a "fast life." Columbia had posed him at the barbecue pit with his cook's apron and hat for a publicity photo, grinning broadly and playing his guitar. He had another photo taken for himself, still with a grin, but wearing a carefully tailored striped suit, a white shirt and white necktie, and a stylishly soft felt hat. He's holding his guitar, but the grin is more of assured success than it is a performer's effort to be agreeable. His face is warm, open, friendly, with deep-set, smiling eyes.

It's easier, in some ways, to understand Charley's relative lack of success than it is to understand Bob's consistent ability to sell records. It was the impression left in their music of the lack of a tradition that limited what they were able to achieve as bluesmen. The music of the black countryside was a functional music, and one of its most important functions was as dance music. Charley's music, and almost as often Bob's, wasn't danceable. They'd worked out a way to add a guitar accompaniment to their singing, but they had trouble fitting all of it into a rhythm, and the guitar followed with its rhythm, and the two halves of the music never quite came together. Bob, at least, worked out some simple guitar strums for accompanying some of his songs, but Charley continued to sing his short vocal line, then followed it with a short guitar figure that sometimes worked against the vocal rhythm. Charley was also a limited guitarist. In some of his pieces, such as "Country Breakdown," he uses two chords, but in most of his blues he only uses one, alternating two rhythmic figures at the same places in the verse. If it had been a music for dancing there would have been a stronger pulse, as there was for the music from Mississippi or from the Carolinas to the north.

Even in the vocal melody there was no feeling of it coming out of a wider dimension. Early black singing was generally in unison, and there were specific rhythmic units shaping the music. Most commentators from the prerecording period stress the communal aspect of the singing, and in most areas of the South there are still elements of the group song in the solo singing that came from it. The most conspicuous example is from Mississippi—the delayed beat of the melody, still allowing time for the fall of the axe that had measured the time of the phrase as it developed out of the work song. Charley and Bob, instead, seem to be singing almost to themselves, with the same kind of introspective, melodic sensitivity that still can be found in the cabin songs from the area. It was a personal expression, with a still plaintiveness, despite its awkwardnesses and hesitations. And there was an assurance to what they did—even if Charley was only playing a one-chord blues with repetitive accompaniment patterns he played it with a strong insistence, and the guitar's twelve strings rang out under his heavy voice. Despite the rhythmic monotony and the limited harmonic color, his performances had their own identity.

Both of the brothers were eclectic in their music—influenced by the recordings they heard and the other singers they hung out with. Bob, because he was a better musician, picked up more than Charley, but Charley often has echoes of other singers in what he does. Each of them assembled verses from other sources, instead of writing new songs. There was some originality—and often they had arresting figures in what they did—but there was little of the inner linking that weaves disparate verse material into a strong emotional fabric. Almost any of Charley's songs shows his difficulties in this area, and the widely distributed "Jealous Hearted Blues" includes almost all of the things he could do, both the aspects of his style that were effective and those that weren't. The song form is the simple narrative blues, with the first line doubled and the third and fourth lines functioning as a refrain that repeats throughout the song. The first verse is a direct, strong statement:

You can have all my money, all I own,
But for God's sake leave my girl alone,
Oh, I'm jealous, jealous, jealous hearted, see,
So jealous, I'm jealous as I can be.

But the second verse, instead of developing this idea—illustrating it or continuing it—falls back on one of the standard erotic verses used in dozens of blues from the period. It could be related to the concept of the first verse—the loss he feels is specifically sexual—but the use of a cliché instead of a verse more directly concerned with the song weakens the effect.

I got a range in my kitchen bakes nice and brown
All I need someone to turn my damper down
'Cause I'm jealous, jealous, jealous hearted, see,
So jealous, I'm jealous as I can be.

The next verse is another standard idea, but the fourth is one of his strongest, and he used it in other blues as well.

I know the mens don't like me 'cause I speaks my mind
Oh the women crazy about me, 'cause I takes my time
Oh, I'm jealous, jealous, jealous hearted, see,
So jealous, I'm jealous as I can be.

The sexual boast implicit in the verse has little relationship to the point where the song started, but it still has its own vividness; it is something you remember him saying. The rest of the song continues with overused verse material, and the effect of the song's strongest material is weakened in the context.

Charley, however, had effective moments as a bluesman despite his limitations. His voice was dark and plaintive, the rhythmic uncertainties of the Atlanta vocal style intensifying the mood of emotional vulnerability. Even in his sexual assertiveness he sounds like a man who could be hurt emotionally, and verses like the "I know the mens don't like me" are strengthened by this sense of unhappy bewilderment. There are moments in each of his blues where his limitations—the awkward guitar accompaniments, the pleading inflection of the voice, the diffuse verse structure—work to make the emotion more deeply expressive.

Bob, with his ability to use other singers' material, had a much broader range than his older brother. His sister remembers that he spent his time with the other Atlanta musicians, Curley Weaver, Buddy Moss, and Willie McTell, and he was conscious of the trends and the styles that were popular at the moment he was scheduled to record. He was consistently able to write songs like his "Mississippi Heavy Water Blues" that mirrored the mood of the blues audience. Often the texts were the same loose assemblages of worn verse material, but sometimes he was able to create a strong blues text. There was a vividness and a directness in the text to "Mississippi Heavy Water Blues."

I was walking down the levee with my head hangin' low,
Lookin' for my sweet mama but she ain't here no mo',
That's why I'm cryin', Mississippi Heavy Water Blues.

I'm sittin' here lookin' at all this mud,
My gal got washed away in that Mississippi flood,
That's why I'm cryin', Mississippi Heavy Water Blues.

I think I heard her moan on that Arkansas side,
Cryin' how long before sweet mama ride,
That's why I'm cryin', Mississippi Heavy Water Blues. . . .

He was a more versatile guitarist than his brother, though he played in a style that was as individual and often as arhythmic.

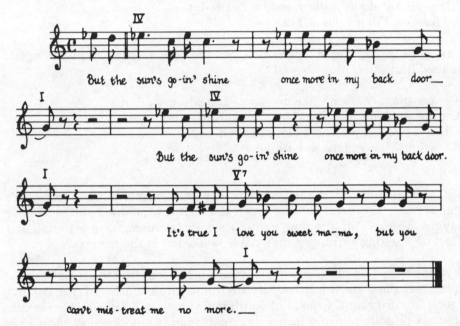

But the sun's go-in' shine once more in my back door

But the sun's go-in' shine once more in my back door.

It's true I love you sweet ma-ma, but you

can't mis-treat me no more.

Both of them had a unique harmonic innovation in the opening phrase of a verse. In many of the songs the guitar continued to strum the chord ending the previous verse through the middle of the new first line—then the rhythm paused and the chord changed to a subdominant harmony, with the voice continuing its phrase. There was also a strong modal sense in much of what Bob sang, even when it was material he seems to have gotten from someone else. It would also seem clear that Frank Walker influenced his choice of material to some extent—there are thin songs that seem to have been recorded only as momentary entertainment. His borrowings from other singers are often almost entirely masked by the uniqueness of his own style. A verse like

Uumh, uumh, lord, lord, lord
Uumh, uumh, lord, lord, lord
You women in Atlanta treated me like a dog

from "She's Gone Blues " has some of the assertiveness and the vocal phrasing of Willie McTell, but these elements have been almost absorbed into his own guitar playing and his own melodic forms. He didn't play twelve-string guitar on all his sessions—"She's Gone Blues" was recorded on a six-string instrument—but his accompaniment style was the same on either type of guitar. In "She's Gone Blues" there's no steady pulse in the accompaniment—only an understated vocal rhythmic unit. The guitar is almost silent when he sings, then it answers the voice in a jumping figure, alternating notes two octaves apart.

Certainly he was effective as an entertainer, whatever limitations he had as a musician. He had new songs ready for more than twenty different sessions, and he did fifty-six blues during his short career. His voice was young and rough, but with a sensitive appeal. Whatever he wanted to sing about came across on the recordings with a freshness and immediacy. He had the ability to communicate, and in a popular song form this is the strongest requirement. When he had a strong song the performance was often hard and exciting. His "Yo Yo Blues" was one of his best later recordings, and it was a brilliant train blues, the accompaniment played with a knife on the strings. There were suggestions of train whistles in the accompaniment, and the song rattled along with a hopping syncopation similar to the older jig rhythm. The verses themselves weren't exceptionally original, but the last line repeated itself in an interesting way.

Hey Mister conductor, let me ride your train
Hey Mister conductor, let me ride your train
I want to clear your yard,
Clear your yard,
Clear your yard again.

You don't let me on I'm goin' ride the blinds
You don't let me on I'm goin' ride the blinds
You wants to yo-yo, Bob, but you know this train,
You know this train ain't mine.

But the last months of 1929 hit Bob just as they hit every other blues artist. As he said in the title of a blues he recorded in April 1930, "We Sure Got Hard Times Now." The same day—April 18—Charley did his last Columbia session, "Doodle Hole Blues" and "Mama Don't Rush Me." They did their minstrel show duets the next week, on April 23. There was a last session for Bob the next December, in which he did six songs. The last of the material was released on Columbia 14614 on August 31, 1931, "It Just Won't Quit" and "Ease It to Me Blues." It was as strong as many of his earlier records, although it sold only 800 copies, and sold is perhaps not the word to use. The copies were pressed and shipped, but most of them probably sat in forgotten bins in half-empty general merchandise stores around the South.

Despite the sales figures, however, Bob had a wide audience, and he would have gone on recording as soon as the worst of the crisis had passed, but he became seriously ill in the fall of 1931. He died in October of pneumonia, already weakened by influenza. His sister thought it could have been tuberculosis, and she felt his hard living had aggravated it, but it seems to have been the combination of the two diseases that killed him. He was twenty-nine years old when he died. For Charley, it meant the end of the small world around him. He'd been so close to his younger brother that he couldn't think of going on with his old life. He stopped playing the guitar and doesn't seem to have played or sung again. The sudden laughter that had marked his records—and given him his name, Laughing Charley—ended. His sister said that he was an alcoholic for many years, and a researcher working in Atlanta, Bruce Bastin, learned that he was jailed in March 1956, when he was living on Old Wheat Street in one of Atlanta's roughest districts. He died in the state penitentiary in September 1963.

Blind Willie McTell, late 1920's.

13.
Willie McTell

I growed up down in south Georgia. Statesboro, Georgia, was my real home. I was born in Tompkins, Georgia, 134 miles from Atlanta, 67 miles west of Augusta. . . . I taken up music when I were quite a child, but in a period of time I quit for eight years. After the eight years I went back to playing as I entered into blind school, Macon, Georgia. I continued my playing up until 19 & 27, the 18th day of October, when I made records for the Victor record people, and from then up until 1932 I played for the Victor people, alone, by myself. But in the period of time, in 1929, I made records for the Columbia people, changing my name to Blind Samuel, and was the author of the song "Come Around to My House, Mama," "Cigaret Blues," and "Atlanta Strut," and so on. And after then I worked with the Vocalion people of 19 & 33, takin' up odd jobs payin' you a small sum of money of $50 a week, but they was getting all the records of blues that they can. And after the period of time I picked up another job with the Decca Record Company. They wanted the blues. They give you a small sum of money, but you get paid expenses. And after the period of time I returned back to Augusta, Georgia, where they had moved the machine, where they laid a gang of blues there in the summer, in June of 1936, and after the period of time I haven't made any more records, but I have lots to be released. . . .

transcribed from an interview with John Lomax, 1940

Probably most country bluesmen would have summed up their careers as laconically as Willie McTell, though they usually didn't have as accurate a memory for dates. But behind the bare outline of McTell's career is the reality of McTell himself, one of the great classic bluesmen. It was true, literally, that he always did have "lots to be released," up to the day of his death in the middle or late

121

fifties. He managed to get himself recorded, he managed to have songs ready for session after session from the fall of 1927 until almost thirty years later, when he did a last group of songs for an Atlanta record store operator in 1956. Thanks to his persistence and his readiness to get into the studio whenever there was a chance to do something, we have an almost unparalleled chance to study the whole career of one of the most gifted bluesmen of the Atlanta school.

Not much more than the simple outline he gave John Lomax is known of his early life; only a few details have been added. He was born on May 5, 1901, and lived in the country until he was nine, when he and his mother moved into Statesboro, Georgia, a small city about halfway between Augusta and Savannah. It's hot, wet country, stifling in the summers and often muggy and oppressive in mid-winter. He wasn't blind from birth, but seems to have become progressively blind in his late teens. Ed Rhoades, an Atlanta record shop owner who met him in 1956, said that McTell had suffered from inflammation of the optic nerve which led to retinal detachment. He had increasing difficulty with his sight, then woke up one morning and everything was black.

Although he told Lomax that he took up traveling with the shows after he left blind school, he seems to have spent most of his teens wandering through rural Georgia with every kind of traveling show. He was most closely associated with the John Roberts Plantation Show in 1916 and 1917, but there's no way of knowing exactly what he did, since he was probably too young to do more than help out and play an occasional number. He was in and out of Statesboro, but still seems to have thought of it as his home until 1920, when his mother died and he moved to Atlanta. As he described those years himself, "I could go anywhere I wanted then without letting anybody know where I was—I didn't have nobody to write back to but a brother, three years old—and he wasn't able to understand."

It's difficult to sort out exactly what he was doing in the twenties, but it could have been during this time that he gave up playing for some time, and he certainly went to schools for the blind, in Michigan and New York, as well as in Georgia. All this suggests that total blindness came in his teens, forcing him to give up his wandering, and he tried to find some other means of support by studying in the blind schools until the popularity of the blues in the mid-twenties brought him back to music.

For whatever reasons McTell wasn't among the first group of Atlanta bluesmen to record. Perhaps he was still out of the city—or perhaps Frank Walker didn't think he'd sell. It was Ralph Peer who finally decided to record him in the fall of 1927, nearly a year after Walker had done the first Atlanta blues recordings with Peg Leg Howell. Peer had started with Victor at the beginning of the year, and he'd made his first trip to Atlanta, where he'd done a lot of recording in the early twenties for OKeh. He was in the city in February, and then when he returned in the fall he recorded McTell on Tuesday, October 18. There were four songs, "Writin' Paper Blues," "Stole Rider Blues," "Mama, 'Tain't Long fo' Day," and "Mr. McTell Got the Blues." When Peer was in Atlanta the following year, on October 17, 1928, there were four more songs recorded,

"Three Women Blues," "Dark Night Blues," "Love Talking Blues," and his well-known "Statesboro Blues." McTell went on recording after this, and there were dozens of blues and a long series of sessions, but he never again was able to sustain the mood of creative intensity that marked these first recordings. There were occasional moments later, scattered masterpieces in otherwise undistinguished sessions, but he seemed to find a peak of expression on these two days of recording in Atlanta.

It's impossible to say why McTell's music was so brilliantly honed in those sessions. It could have been a kind of young intensity; it could have been Peer himself, who worked slowly with artists when he was out with the Victor field unit, usually recording only a handful of sides during a day's work. Songs were timed in the studio, there were rehearsals, there was a chance for someone like McTell, recording for the first time, to get the feel of what he was doing. And Peer seemed to like singers with an individual style, who gave their blues a distinctive mood or form. Frank Walker, on the other hand, liked the rough and tumble of his country recordings, and he liked noisy country humor. When Walker took McTell into the studio on October 30 and 31, 1929, two years after his first Victor sessions, McTell recorded syncopated guitar pieces, medicine show songs, and talking blues. It could also have been that Walker was trying to give McTell some kind of direction. No sales figures are available, but there's nothing to indicate that his blues for Peer sold very well. McTell was recorded only once a year and only when Victor happened to be in Atlanta to do something else. With Columbia he began to make an effort to keep up with current trends, and he went on making the same effort for the rest of his career. Perhaps it was Frank Walker who was responsible for the change, perhaps it was McTell himself. There's no way, now, to tell.

But the first blues that he did—and the occasional masterpieces that he did in scattered sessions later—what was it in them that made them so unique? For the earliest sessions it was the plaintive quality of his singing voice that was immediately identifiable. His voice was high and rather light, sounding much younger than someone in his late twenties, and there was almost a pleading quality to it, a helplessness to his phrasing. He strengthened the impression with verses that emphasized his drifting and his homelessness. In "Statesboro Blues" he begins:

> Wake up mama, turn your lamp down low,
> Wake up mama, turn your lamp down low.
> Have you got the nerve to drive Papa McTell from your door?

The second verse, where he seems to be asserting his independence and his ability with women, only makes his vulnerability more evident since he says that he's orphaned and, even if he has a woman, he's already said in the first verse that he isn't staying with her.

> My mother died and left me reckless, my daddy died and left me
>   wild, wild, wild,

Mother died and left me reckless, daddy died and left me
   wild, wild, wild.
Now I ain't good lookin' but I'm some sweet woman's angel child.

The third verse continues with his mood of unhappiness:

She's a mighty mean woman, do me this-a way. . . .

And the fourth suggests that whatever good things have happened to him were at some other time, in some other place.

I once loved a woman better than any'n I ever seen,
I once loved a woman better than any'n I ever seen.
Treated me like I was a king and she was a doggone queen.

All of these things had been included in dozens of blues, but there was something in his voice that made it seem reasonable that the song at least came close to his own experience. All of this was accompanied with a restless, busy guitar background, with modal elements, and a sense of irresolution to what he was doing, as if he felt he had to keep hurrying on after something.

There was the same restlessness in the great "Mama, 'Tain't Long fo' Day," played with a slide on the six-string guitar he used for the first session in October 1927. It began with him again waking up a woman.

Wake up mama, don't you sleep so hard,
Wake up mama, don't you sleep so hard.
For it's these old blues walkin' all over your yard.

The person he described in this blues is the same one that he described in "Statesboro Blues."

Blues grabbed me at midnight, didn't turn me loose 'til day,
Blues grabbed me at midnight, didn't turn me loose 'til day.
I didn't have no mama to drive these blues away.

He follows the vocal melody with the slide melody on the guitar, still picking the bass strings with his thumb. The contrasts in the accompaniment seem to mirror his uncertainty as passages played with the slide alternate with measures of finger-picking on the lower strings. In one of the most beautiful verses, the guitar picks up a phrase at the end of the first line and repeats it with a kind of emotional extension that heightens the poignancy of his singing.

The big star fallin' mama tain't long fo' day.
The big star fallin' mama tain't long fo' day.
Maybe the sunshine'll drive these blues away.

Since these are the kinds of effects and the kind of mood that Peer got from many singers, it could have been his influence that gave the music some of its quality, and certainly McTell never did it consistently again although he continued to create occasional remarkable performances throughout his career.

It was also his guitar playing that was distinctively his own in these two early sessions. Certainly he used figures and patterns he'd taken from the recordings of Blind Blake and Blind Lemon Jefferson, but he wove them into a shifting, continually fascinating pattern. He's often been described as "free" in his musical approach, but this is an oversimplification. His singing generally remained in the standard blues patterns, and the harmonic changes are the standard I-IV-V 12-bar verse. Usually the guitar part accompanying the singing was also consistent and fairly regular. It was the extension phrases at the end of the line that were unpredictable in their form, even if the voice usually came in with the next line correctly in rhythm. Also between verses he often varied the bridge material both in length and style. On the Victor sessions, where he had time to work everything out, there is a highly effective tension between the regularity of the voice and the unpredictability of the guitar, and, since everything he played still had his own characteristic sound, the musical texture that resulted was very effective. In later sessions, where he doesn't seem to have had much time, the final result was often jumbled and unclear.

The change from six-string to twelve-string guitar between the first two sessions didn't seem to make much difference in his style. He was one of the few guitarists who could handle the more cumbersome twelve-string instrument with the same case as the simpler guitar. But there was a wiry astringency to the sound of the twelve-string that also emphasized the plaintiveness of the voice. He usually played in standard tunings, most often in the keys of C and E, and retuned to open E for the pieces he played with a slide.

During this period of his life he was one of the crowd of young blues musicians hanging out on Decatur Street. He knew the Hicks brothers well, and he was close to Buddy Moss and Curley Weaver, a younger musician who worked with him on his later sessions in the thirties. McTell was a short, slight man, about 5'8", and in the one photograph of him from this period—his Victor publicity photo—he was in a suit and vest, with a watch chain, a white shirt and a necktie. He has a cap on over his boyish face, and he has a small moustache. He seems very small and very young, and the large Stella twelve-string guitar on his lap makes him look even smaller.

After the two sessions with Ralph Peer, released under the name Blind Willie McTell, Columbia became interested in him. In 1929 Walker was in Atlanta a month before the Victor unit got to town and recorded six songs on October 30 and 31. The first, "Travelin' Blues" and "Come on Around to My House Mama," was released on Columbia's 14000 race series, Col 14484-D, on January 3, 1930. Probably to avoid difficulties with Victor, the record was released under the name of Blind Sammie, the first of what was to be many pseudonyms for Willie. Columbia's allocation system was still functioning, despite the financial crisis, and the initial distribution for the record was 2205 copies, with a repressing of 2000, about standard for a lesser known artist at this point. A month later Peer was in Atlanta and did eight titles on November 26 and 29, but only two were released, "Drive Away Blues" and "Love-Changing Blues." Columbia was interested in him enough to do another session in April 1930, then, despite the financial pinch, recorded him on October 23 and 31 in 1931. His last two Columbia releases were transferred to the OKeh label, which had become a Columbia subsidiary, and he was given a new name, "Georgia Bill."

The Columbia sessions were mixed, musically and stylistically. There were some great blues, like "Broke Down Engine Blues" and "Scarey Day Blues," there were some racially distasteful medicine show numbers like "Razor Ball," some loosely shaped ragtime pieces, and some rather disorganized blues that showed more and more influence from other recordings. Clearly there's a groping for some kind of identity, and despite the moments of brilliance there's no sign that McTell ever found it. Walker says that he was responsible for choosing what he would record of an artist's repertoire; so it could have been his own indecision that caused the recordings to drift so perceptibly. But "Broke Down Engine Blues" was one of McTell's masterpieces, and he recorded it again at other sessions over the next twenty years.

The record was shipped to retailers on December 15, 1931, but the initial pressing was only 500 copies and there was no additional pressing order. It's difficult to say whether his records were reaching any kind of audience, since sales by all artists had reached the same grim levels. A Bessie Smith recording was released the same month with a pressing of only 800 copies for a "special release," and there was a note in the files to the production department: ". . . Manufacture against shipping orders only." He kept going, though, with the same kind of gritty determination that marked his long and tangled career. He and a woman named Ruby Glaze did four party blues for Victor on February 22, 1932. They were similar in structure to the blues that Lonnie Johnson had been doing with Clara Smith and Victoria Spivey. The woman sang the first lines:

> Oh, roll me on my belly, babe, feed me with your chocolate stuff
>   (McTell answers in the background, "I'll feed you with it, baby.")
> Oh, roll me on my belly, babe, feed me with your chocolate stuff
>   ("I'll give it all to you, mama.")

And McTell finished the verse:

> I want you to keep it all for your daddy and don't give nobody none.

There seem to be two guitars playing the rather heavy accompaniments, stylistically very similar to the duets he was to do the next year with Curley Weaver, but both guitars sound like twelve-strings and Weaver usually played a six-string.

The sessions the next year were for the newly reorganized Brunswick Radio Corporation and were released on Vocalion label, although of the twenty-three songs he did only twelve were finally issued. He went to New York with a group of Atlanta artists, including Curley Weaver, who sang and played with him on some of the dates, and Buddy Moss, who seems to have accompanied him on another of the sessions. Vocalion records sold for thirty-five cents, and they had a much better chance at the little market that was left than Columbia or Victor, whose records were still priced at seventy-five cents. The pressing quality was generally poor, and the sessions were hurried, but the difference in price was enough of a compensation for the average purchaser, who had very little money for anything by this time. McTell recorded on September 14, 18, 19, and 21, and redid two of his strongest songs for Columbia, "Broke Down Engine" and "Southern Can Mama," as well as a broad spectrum of other material, including, for the first time, religious songs.

The struggle for a clear identity was even more acute than it had been for his Columbia sessions between 1929 and 1931. By this time the music of the country male blues artists had become as much a standard commercial product as the urban blues of the women singers had become in the late 1920s, and there was a need for a singer to find a kind of self-projection that related to the concerns of the record buyer. It was the need for a kind of persona that Memphis Minnie, among others, had been so successful in projecting. McTell, clearly, had no strong identification with this kind of blues. His singing, during these sessions, was pleasant and musical, but not characterized by any strong emotion, and the two guitar duets were generally a little cumbersome. The strongest influence on him now seemed to be Lonnie Johnson as a blues singer and Blind Willie Johnson as a gospel singer. Blues like "Death Cell Blues" show the Lonnie Johnson influence even in the guitar playing. McTell seems to have absorbed almost all of Johnson's characteristic figures. The gospel songs were played in an open tuning with a slide, and there was a rough power to them, but they were disorganized and too similar to the Blind Willie Johnson records that were still somewhat popular. "Lord Have Mercy If You Please" and "Don't You See How This World Made a Change" were released on Vocalion 02623, with Curley Weaver playing the second guitar and joining him for the singing.

The Vocalion labels and the various A.R.C. labels were now under the control of the Consolidated Film Industries, who had bought out the two parent companies in 1930 and 1931, and if there had been any strong response to the Vocalion releases there probably would have been an effort made to get McTell into a studio again, but they let him go to Decca, an American subsidiary of the English Decca operation, which started its thirty-five-cent blues label in 1934. Decca's recording was under the direction of Jack Kapp, who had been the head of the old Vocalion race series, and he also brought with him Mayo Williams, who'd been working with him before in Chicago. They were interested in getting as much material as possible, and in 1935 they brought Willie to Chicago, where he recorded on April 23 and 25. His wife Kate was with him for these sessions, and the gospel duets they did are even more influenced by Blind Willie Johnson than were the duets he'd done with Curley Weaver two years before. There is some possibility that Kate McTell is the same woman who recorded the blues duets with him for Victor as Ruby Glaze, but their voices, while similar, seem to reflect different levels of professionalism, and they seem to be separate artists. Kate's contribution to the records was the kind of responsive vocal chorus that Angeline Johnson, and others, had added to Blind Willie Johnson's records.

It's certainly possible that Mayo Williams was influential in the sound of gospel recordings that McTell made. They were released under the name Blind Willie, with as much of Johnson's style as possible, and the idea may have been to convince some buyers that this was the original Blind Willie Johnson. All of the companies had begun a policy of doing only a single take of each number, which also worked to McTell's disadvantage, since he often was undecided about the structure of his pieces. Curley Weaver was with him for these sessions, and—as in New York—he did some solo pieces of his own, including "Tricks Ain't Walkin' No More." On the blues that McTell did, the Lonnie Johnson influence was even stronger on some pieces, like "Bell Street Blues," which had the same kind of careful literalness that marked all of Lonnie's recordings during this period.

> . . . That Bell Street whiskey make you sleep all in your clothes,
> That old Bell Street whiskey make you sleep all in your clothes,
> And when you wake up next mornin' feel like you done laid outdoors.
>
> I drank so much Bell Street whiskey they won't sell McTell no more,
> I drank so much Bell Street whiskey won't sell poor boy McTell no more.
> I've got the cans and glasses, boys, layin' all 'round my door.

The last session also included blues like "Cold Winter Day," in the style of Memphis Minnie, and there was almost an obsessiveness with death in the last titles, among them, "Lay Some Flowers on My Grave," "Death Room Blues," "Dying Doubler Blues," and "Cooling Board Blues," the last a reference to the "board" where a body was laid after death.

The Decca sessions seem to have been as poor in sales as the Vocalion sessions, and the company didn't record him again. But in October 1940, he was recorded by John Lomax for the Library of Congress Archives in an Atlanta hotel room, and the interviews and music he did that morning are a priceless glimpse of McTell as an artist. Lomax had been told about him by friends and only a short time later his wife noticed McTell at one of the "Little Pig" barbecue stands that they passed in their car. They stopped and asked him if he wanted to come to the hotel and he answered, "Business isn't so good, I'll go along with you to your hotel." Lomax couldn't remember the location of the hotel, but, as he remembered: " 'I'll show you,' said totally blind Willie. Between us and the hotel there were six or eight right-angled cross streets and two places where five or six streets crossed. Chatting all the while with me, Blind Willie called every turn, even mentioning the location of the stoplights. He gave the names of buildings as we passed them. Stored in his mind was an accurate detailed photograph of Atlanta."

McTell agreed to come back early the next morning and record for a dollar and cab fare, and he did a variety of material, from gospel songs to folk ballads, as well as some blues and the sketch of his life. Much of what he sang probably was at Lomax's request, since it's similar to the kind of material that the Library of Congress was looking for. But thanks to the monologs, the session did give a sense of McTell as a person, and there was also the first version he was to do of his song "Dying Crapshooter's Blues." This personal reworking of the old "Streets of Laredo" theme is one of McTell's masterpieces, and this version, which seems to have been recorded not long after he wrote it, since he didn't do it on earlier sessions, has a clarity of musical detail that the two later versions lack, even though the 1949 version recorded for Atlantic Records has the best sound of the three. McTell described it to Lomax as his own composition. "I am goin' play this song that I made myself, originated it from Atlanta. It's three different marches of tunes." The tempo is more relaxed than it became later, and all the details of the accompaniment are brilliantly clear. The gospel material was similar to what he'd been recording for the commercial companies, but the whole morning's recording was a clear portrait of McTell and his music. When he'd finished he wouldn't let Lomax call a cab, saying he'd just have that more money, and he set off from the hotel walking through the Atlanta streets he knew so well.

The wartime boom hit Georgia, just as it hit every other part of the country, but McTell was forty, and his music wasn't close enough to any kind of pop style for him to work in the local nightclubs. He sang for occasional parties, worked the streets singing for tips, and often went out to the Sea Islands to play for tourists in the summers. He was still with Kate, and the local office of the Lighthouse for the Blind seems to have begun helping him during this period. He did a lot of his playing in the crowded parking lots outside the nightclubs, and he was also a regular at the chain of Pig 'N' Whistle stands.

During all of this period he and Curley Weaver were still playing together, and he was still known as a blues artist; so it was only to be expected that the new labels looking for material in the postwar years would pick him up again. Atlantic Records did an extended session with him in 1949, after their Atlanta distributor had told Ahmet Ertegun—who with his brother Nesuhi had started the company in 1947—about McTell. It was one of McTell's more interesting sessions, with songs ranging from a wonderful new version of his "Broke Down Engine Blues" to some country ragtime, a second recording of "Dying Crapshooter's Blues," and some gospel pieces. Fifteen titles were recorded, but only two were released at the time, "Broke Down Engine Blues" and "Kill It Kid," which he'd recorded for Lomax as "Kill-It-Kid Rag." They came out on a 78, Atlantic 891, under still another pseudonym, "Barrelhouse Sammy (The Country Boy)."

The same year he also recorded more of his standard repertoire for Regal Records, a small independent company operating in New Jersey. He and Weaver traveled together to the sessions, and Curley did some solo things of his own at the same time, including his "Tricks Ain't Walkin' No More," which came out as "Trixie" on the Sittin' In With label. The material that came out on the Regal and Savoy labels was under still different names, "Pig 'N' Whistle Band," "Pig 'N' Whistle Red," as well as "Blind Willie" and his own name, the last two used for gospel material. As with the Atlantic session not everything was used, and the rest didn't appear until years afterward.

The pattern that had developed in McTell's relationship with other companies— a large group of songs recorded as part of a new blues line—repeated itself again, and there was no follow-up to any of the releases. He was still singing and playing as brilliantly as ever, but his style never caught on with the young blues audience, which was looking for something with more obvious theatricality. McTell's individuality and personal intensity obviously put some people off.

It got harder and harder for him to scuffle a living. People who saw him in the 1950s remember him as a short, stocky, grizzled man, always with his big Stella twelve-string, making his own way around Atlanta's streets. But there was to be a final session. In August 1956, a young Atlanta record shop operator named Ed Rhoades was playing blues records in the shop one night and some-one said, "There's a guy like that singing in the alley." It was McTell, singing in the parking lot of the Blue Lantern on Ponce de Leon.

For the next few months McTell stopped by the store regularly. Rhoades remembers that he was often drunk and that he would drink anything anyone offered him. He was still dressed with the same kind of formality he'd had for his Victor portrait, and the photos Ed took of him show him in a suit jacket and a tie. At this point he was living in a cellar in a house two doors down from the Coconut Grill. He was still playing Stella twelve-strings, and if he broke one he always got a new one. In the fall of 1956 Ed decided to record him, and he sat him down in front of a tape recorder and asked him to sing for friends. What he got was McTell's street repertoire, from "Basin Street Blues" to "The Wabash Cannonball," but, as always, there were sudden moments of brilliance, like "Dying Crapshooter Blues" and still another version of "Kill it Kid," and the tapes are an invaluable last glimpse into the world of Willie McTell, including some introductions to the songs and some information about his own life.

In the spring of the next year Rhoades remembers that McTell began to lose his voice. His wife, a woman named Helen now, was in poor health, and McTell was receiving help from The Lighthouse for the Blind on a regular basis. Rhoades lost touch with them and heard later that she died in 1959 and McTell a year later, in October 1960, though no death certificate has been found—only a file card from The Lighthouse with the word "deceased" written across it. The tapes from the session sat in a closet in Rhoades's store, with other things in a cardboard box, and he had almost forgotten about them until he read *The Country Blues* about the same time McTell died. He flew to New York in 1961 with the tapes and we listened together on a worn Pentron tape recorder in a dark apartment on West 72nd street. The tapes were sad to hear, despite the insight they gave into McTell's last years as an artist, because they showed so clearly how little he had been able to use his great blues talent in his years of street entertaining. For Rhoades they had a particular poignance, for he was suffering from the same eye trouble that had blinded McTell, and as his own sight got worse he felt closer and closer to his memory of McTell. The songs were brought out by Prestige on their Bluesville series.

Willie McTell must be regarded as one of the great blues artists for the brilliant and sensitive musicality of his first sessions and for the scattered masterpieces that he was able to record over the next twenty-five years. Like all of the Atlanta men he had to struggle with the lack of a strongly defined local blues style to give his music a direction, but in a way more than the others he was able to develop a style that was often eclectic, but at its best moments fused all the elements into a direct and strong emotional statement. The thing that's important about the body of music McTell left behind isn't that much of it is weak— the important thing is that he created a handful of blues that are among the most moving of all the early country blues.

Blind Willie McTell, 1956.

14.
Some Other Atlanta Singers

Most of the recording done in Atlanta was with white artists, and the recording of black music tended to concentrate on a relative handful of singers, but there were occasional other bluesmen who did record in Atlanta and there were also local men who managed to have a recording career despite the difficulty in interesting the companies there. Sometimes the Atlanta facilities were used to record singers from other areas, and musicians like Barefoot Bill and Pillie Bolling were brought in from Alabama for Columbia's 14000 series, and Bo Chatman was brought from Mississippi for OKeh. Peer even brought the Memphis Jug Band to Atlanta to record in October 1927. But there were also some recordings that seem to be by men singing along Decatur Street, even though they weren't part of the group around the Hicks brothers. In November 1927, Frank Walker recorded a singer named Emery Glen, and he sounds like an older man who had been close to the Atlanta blues style. There were four sides, "Back Door Blues" and "Blue Blazes Blues" on Columbia 14472, and "Two Ways to Texas" and "Fifth Street Blues" on Columbia 14283, all recorded on November 7. Despite the reference to Texas in the title of one of the blues, there are marked similarities to the other Atlanta men. He's playing a twelve-string guitar and there's the same kind of vocal phrase, with the guitar filling out the rhythmic unit in a kind of strum. His texts, however, were a kind of stage theatrical diction—mixed with more usual blues verses.

> I got the blue, blue blazes blues, it burns all night long,
> I got the blue, blue blazes blues, it burns all night long,
> I sits up wonderin' because my good gal's gone.
>
> Smoke go up the chimney, black clouds hangin' low,
> Smoke goes up the chimney, black clouds hangin' low.
> Where in the world did my good gal go?

Papa love mama, mama do love me,
Papa love mama, mama do love me,
Mama's in the graveyard, papa's in the pen.

You will have the blue, blue blazes blues, it burns all night long,
If you had treated your good gal wrong,
Well, you can't mistreat 'em, why she left me no one ever know.

Nothing is known of Glen except for these four sides he recorded on one of Columbia's trips to Atlanta.

One of the most interesting artists to record with some of the Atlanta style in what he sang was Willie Baker, who recorded for Gennett in Richmond, Indiana, in 1929. He did considerable recording, and there were six sessions between January 9 and March 11. For some reason Gennett recorded his first four songs over and over—two of them, "Weak-Minded Blues" and "Sweet Patunia Blues," were recorded four different times—so there were only eight blues, but they are an interesting musical group. "Weak-Minded Blues" was almost pure Hicks— with the same halting rhythms and vocal phrasing that made Barbecue Bob's records so distinctive, even though Baker was singing verses that had been done earlier by singers like Blind Lemon Jefferson, including the well-known "I wonder will a matchbox , mama, hold my dirty clothes. . . ." Something like "Rag Baby," on the other hand, was an older eight-bar blues with almost a sentimental minstrel show harmonic form and a kind of sentimental text, using only bits of phrases like:

I have a baby,
You have a baby,
I ain't got no baby now.

And this was played with a kind of early finger-picking style that gathered momentum as he hurried through it.

Walker had recorded Eddie Anthony with Peg Leg Howell's gang and even had him sing on some violin/guitar duets Howell and Anthony did together in 1928, but Anthony appeared under his own name—at least as Macon Ed—on OKeh, recording with titles like "Tantalizing Bootblack" and "Warm Wipe Stomp." Since OKeh was under the general umbrella of Columbia at this time, the sessions may have been supervised by Walker, and the Tampa Joe, who played guitar with Macon Ed on the sessions, could even have been Howell, though there isn't a great stylistic similarity between these duets and the solo records Howell was doing at this time.

There were also younger men who were part of the scene, and their recording careers began later, among them Buddy Moss, who became one of the most important figures in the development of the Piedmont blues; the harmonica player Eddie Mapp, who recorded with Curley Weaver; Fred McMullen, who went on to New York to record with Weaver and Ruth Willis in January 1933;

and Weaver himself, who was a close friend of Blind Willie McTell's and had a lengthy recording career of his own. Little is known of McMullen, and Mapp was found murdered in an Atlanta street in 1931, at the age of twenty. Weaver began his career under the shadow of Barbecue Bob, and his first session, for Frank Walker, included a "No No Blues" that was very close, stylistically, to what Bob Hicks was doing.

It isn't surprising that they should have been close musically, since they had known each other for many years. Weaver, whose first name was James, was born in 1906 not far from the Hicks brothers and knew both of them before he moved into Atlanta in 1925. Weaver's other recordings were not so close to the Atlanta style, and he had become a Piedmont guitarist by the time he did his last session—for Regal Records in New Jersey in 1949. He was closely associated with McTell in the 1930s and worked with him on many of his sessions for A.R.C. He himself had some success with his version of the well-known "Tricks Ain't Walkin' No More," which he recorded under various names both for A.R.C. and for Regal. It was his first recording—the "No No Blues" on Columbia 14386, recorded on October 26, 1928—that was most fully in the Atlanta style, but there was a suggestion of the city's sound in many of the songs he did over the next twenty years. He was not a distinctive artist. He had a pleasant voice, not strongly individual, but his singing and his guitar playing were skillful and musical, and his music is an important addition to the story of the blues in Atlanta.

The Atlantic Coast and the Carolinas

15.
The Atlantic Coast and the Carolinas

The southern Atlantic Coast is the old coast line of North America—flat, swampy, a bedraggled stretch of trees, dunes, and mud. The coast is slowly sinking as the movements of the earth's crust pull it toward the west while the California coast rises higher behind its steep line of cliffs. As the level falls the ocean seeps into the hundreds of stream beds and shallow indentations in the shoreline, and the coast of the Carolinas or Georgia, up into Virginia, is a maze of twisting, stagnant tidal waterways and low islands. The land slowly rises, flattening across the alluvial plains of North Carolina and South Carolina, the Tidewater flatlands of Virginia and Maryland; then it heaves into lines of stony ridge, then into the raw wilderness of the Appalachian Mountains, dark and wood-covered in a sweeping mass hovering above the rolling inland country behind the coast.

The first settlements in the South were scattered along the coast—at first on the small islands themselves, but they were too disease-ridden, and the people surviving the fevers pushed their way inland along the banks of the rivers. The first Africans were brought to America to the coastal islands in 1622, only a short time after the first Europeans had arrived, and the two races grew up together in the new environment. Despite the differences in their status, they influenced each other in a complex interrelationship.

The coastal islands are still beautiful in their fringed cloak of trees and moss and the silences of their winding waterways, but they no longer have a dominant position in the culture of the area. Most of the people have left—except for growing clusters of summer vistors—and the people left from the older period have lost much of their distinctiveness. Only in the Georgia Sea Islands is there still a unique culture—the Geechee and Gullah cultures surviving from the pre-Civil War slavery period. It was the land away from the coast—which was turned to tobacco and cotton culture—that played a large role in the development of the blues, but along the coastal stretch the music had its own characteristics.

The blues of the Virginia and Carolina areas seem, in some respects, to reflect an earlier musical tradition than the blues that emerged from the Mississippi Delta. The earliest importation of slaves had been to these colonies, and the roots of Afro-American culture had been shaped here among the Mandingo and Wolof peoples who found themselves in the new world. The Wolofs brought the banjo with them—a small wooden instrument with a skin head called the halam— and the Mandingoes brought the playing techniques of their stringed instrument, the kora. The kora is played with an alternating thumb technique, the other strings plucked with the first finger, much as Gary Davis played the guitar. The last three fingers are used to support the instrument. The kora is a large instrument, rather difficult to construct, and requires a large, dried calabash for its body. Probably because of this the instrument didn't survive in the new environment, but the banjo spread rapidly and soon was played by slaves of every tribal group.

The characteristc sound of kora playing is a rather free finger picking, with a rhythmic center in the alternate thumb stroke. It is, however, considerably less structured than the later Carolinas guitar picking. This style first was transmuted to the banjo; then, as the banjo was taken up extensively by whites, the techniques were transferred to the guitar. The European bar line divisions became more clearly defined, and the stressed beat pattern became more dominant, as happened to other styles of African music when they were altered by European influence. By the time the guitar styles fully matured there was probably no real consciousness of an earlier tradition, and most of the musicians, if questioned, would have gone no further back than the banjo as a source for their style. Gary Davis, in fact, regarded it as a personal innovation and told Stefan Grossman he had learned it by listening to local piano players.

Except for the Piedmont guitar school that centered around Buddy Moss, Gary Davis, and Blind Boy Fuller, the recordings of the coastal bluesmen are scattered and inconclusive. They do point, however, to an older style that was dying out by the time recordings were first made in the region. Few of the coastal musicians even recorded in the area. Bayless Rose recorded for Gennett in Richmond, Indiana; William Moore, who was born in Georgia but grew up in Tappahannock, Virginia, recorded for Paramount in Chicago; Willie Walker, from Greenville, South Carolina, was recorded in Atlanta. Only Luke Jordan, who was from Lynchburg, Virginia, was recorded away from one of the major cities for his first session. Peer recorded him in Charlotte, North Carolina, on a field trip in 1927, then brought him to New York for a second session.

The scarcity of recordings by coastal artists probably wasn't simply because the field units missed them—though certainly many fine musicians were missed, despite the efforts of scouts from half a dozen companies. All of the companies were recording white artists in the Virginia and Carolina areas, and they would have recorded bluesmen if they'd found them. The answer seems to be that the coastal style was losing out to other kinds of music, and it was only in the Carolinas that a new style was emerging.

It is difficult to generalize from only a handful of singers and recordings, but certainly there is a unique quality to the coastal music. There was still a strong instrumental tradition, and there were many pieces that were called "rags" in their repertoire. Sylvester Weaver, who was one of the first country bluesmen to be recorded and sounds like a coastal artist, did two instrumental pieces, "Guitar Rag" and "Guitar Blues," for his first OKeh release in 1923. By "rag" what was usually meant was a medium tempo piece with a syncopated picking in eighth notes against a bass line that had many of the alternating thumb characteristics. The pieces generally were not melodic, but instead repeated their little picking patterns over changing chords, and the sense of a melody came from the progression of the chords themselves. There was considerable variety within each performer's "rags," but one of the most widespread chord progressions for rag pieces in the thirties was some variation on:

C — A — D7/G7 — C

One of the formulas used in the Piedmont area was to repeat this phrase twice, then add a bridge going to subdominant harmony:

C — C7 — F — Fm

An entire piece using this progression would be:

C — A (or A7) — D7/G7 — C
C — A — D7 - G7
C — C7 — F — Fm
C — A — D7/G7 — C

Many of the "rags" of singers like Fuller, and even of Chicago artists like Bill Broonzy, were built around it. William Moore's "Barbershop Rag" is a classic example of the chord sequence, with the slight twist of beginning his eight-bar phrase on the A chord; so it becomes:

A — A — D — D
G — G — C — C

This progression is so characteristic of guitar ragtime that it could almost be a definition of a certain kind of piece, just as the twelve-bar blues progression is part of the definition of the blues.

Most of the coastal singers appeared long enough to record, then dropped out of sight again; so not much is known about them. William Moore refers to himself as a barber in his "Barbershop Rag."

Old barber Moore on the box,
Only barber in the world can shave you and give you music
    at the same time. . . .

His Paramount recordings were done around January 1928, when he was in the studio on two different days. The first day he did seven numbers, including "Ragtime Crazy," "Ragtime Millionaire," and "Barbershop Rag." At the next session he did only two numbers, but both of them were instrumentals, "Old Country Rock" and "Raggin' the Blues," released on Paramount 12761. "Old Country Rock" seems to include elements of an even older style, and probably comes out of a kind of banjo—or guitar-banjo duet—style from the pre-blues period. It has a distinctive flavor to it and is one of the most brilliant examples of the genre. Moore lived out the rest of his life in Tappahannock and died there in 1955.

Bayless Rose recorded on two separate days for Gennett in Richmond, Indiana, but of the three pieces recorded the first day, May 24, 1930, two were recorded again on June 7; so his total output was six sides, of which four were never released. He sounds like a country songster who also knew some blues, and his singing and the texts are undistinguished. However, he did an interesting instrumental, "Jamestown Exposition," presumably named after the celebrations for the three-hundred-year anniversary of the founding of the British colony at Jamestown, Virginia. It has the same reflection of earlier banjo playing and refers to the even earlier style of halam and kora playing that the slaves had brought to the coastal colonies. It was released on the same record as his "Frisco Blues," a slide train piece very similar to Furry Lewis's accompaniment style for "John Henry."

Luke Jordan, like Rose, was a songster, but his blues had a beautiful sweetness and a kind of wry wistfulness that made them unforgettable. He was a good guitarist, but his accompaniments were kept simple, to emphasize his texts. His home was in Lynchburg, Virginia, a small city in the mountains. Peer recorded him first in Charlotte, North Carolina, on August 16, 1927, doing two blues, "Church Bells Blues" and "Cocaine Blues," and two minstrel numbers, one a version of a mountain folk song recorded by a number of people, among them Geeshie Wiley, called "Pick Poor Robin Clean." Neither of his blues was in the usual melodic pattern, but the guitar had a softly swinging rhythm, and the voice seemed almost quitely amused at the vagaries he was singing about. He was recorded again more than two years later, when Peer brought him to New York for sessions on November 18 and 19, 1929, but only six songs were recorded, and two were unissued. He returned to Lynchburg after the sessions and lived quietly there, making his living as a songster and working odd jobs.

Other singers from the area who seem to be stylistically related—such as Willie Walker and Pink Anderson, who was from Spartanburg, South Carolina, as well as Carl Martin, who was born in Virginia and moved to Knoxville, Tennessee—are more closely tied to the Piedmont school. The first of the Carolina men to record was Julius Daniels, who, Bruce Bastin learned, was born in 1902 in Denmark, South Carolina, then moved to Pineville, a small community outside Charlotte, North Carolina, when he was ten years old. Ralph Peer may have heard him on one of his trips through the area, and he recorded Daniels in Atlanta. There were two sessions, one on February 19, 1927, with Bubba Lee Torrence singing with him on two sides, and the other on October 24, 1927, with Wilbert Andrews playing second guitar and singing. Even though Daniels was still in his twenties when he recorded, he has the feel of an older songster, and his range of material went from blues like "My Mama Was a Sailor" to gospel songs like "Slippin' and Slidin' Up the Golden Street." His songs themselves reflect this eclecticism, and even his most interesting performances, like his "Crow Jane Blues" on Victor 21065, are more assemblages of other material than distinct personal compositions. His guitar playing already has some of the elements of the Piedmont style, though he never had the fluid rhythmic movement of the musicians who came later. Bastin has also located his death certificate; he died in Pineville from the effects of syphilis on October 8, 1947.

Probably the closest to a legendary figure from this early period of the Piedmont blues is Willie Walker, a blind musician from Greenville, South Carolina. People as diverse as Josh White—who, when he was a boy in Greenville, heard Walker and probably led him through the streets—and Gary Davis—who played with Walker in a string band in Greenville in 1912 and 1913—agree that he was the finest guitarist of them all, and he may have been one of the most facile of the musicians playing in this East Coast style. Walker fortunately was recorded by Frank Walker, and for once the legend and the reality bear each other out. He doesn't have Davis's flaring intensity or Fuller's irresistible swagger, but his technique is stunning. The playing is loosely rhythmic and swinging, with sudden busy runs picked with a startling assurance. Bastin took a copy of the Walker recording to Walker's old neighborhood more than thirty years after his death and found that people still remembered his playing with awe. He was born afflicted with congenital syphilis and was blind from birth. He was the same age as Gary Davis, both of them born in 1896, and came to Greenville when he was still in his teens, probably 1911 or 1912, since Bastin found a listing for the family on Elmford Street in the 1913 City Directory. Most of Walker's playing was in the ragtime style—usually in the key of C—and no one was considered his equal in that key.

Walker always played with another Greenville musician, Sam Brooks, as his second guitarist, and Brooks added an unobtrusive but solid and sensitive background to Walker's playing, leaving Walker free to play his flowing runs. Brooks was a carpenter who came to Greenville about the same time as Walker's family, and he's remembered for always having a large wad of tobacco in his mouth as he played. Both of them went to Atlanta for the Columbia session, recording four titles on December 6, 1930. Of the four only two were released, "South Carolina Rag" and "Dupree Blues," on Columbia 14578. The "South Carolina Rag" is really a little song called "That's No Way to Do," but for Walker the text and the song are almost secondary. He has four verses that he repeats throughout the record, after beginning with a partial verse referring to the guitar playing.

Hey, play that boy.
I want to tell you that's no way to do.

Asked for a drink of water, she brought gasoline.
Now let me tell you, doin' me mighty mean.
I want to tell you that's no way to do.

Talk about your gal, ought to see mine,
She's the sweetest gal in town.
I want to tell you that's no way to do.

Hey, hey, play that thing,
Hey, play that thing.
I want to tell you that's no way to do.

Music man, ain't it grand,
Play that thing, boy, long as you can.
I want to tell you that's no way to do. . . .

Walker was also a fine singer, with a warm, expressive voice, but his concern is certainly not with the text. His "Dupree Blues," on the other side of the record, is a version of "Betty and Dupree," which is more concerned with the story and the guitar playing is more restrained. Harmonically the rag was in the usual four-chord circle—an eight-measure verse of

$$A - A - D - D$$
$$G - G - C - C$$

though sometimes between the two guitars the chords are played in different inversions. It's unfortunate that Walker never had another opportunity to record. He might have had a chance to get into a studio again when the record business began to pick up, but he died of the effects of syphilis on March 3, 1933.

Pink Anderson and Carl Martin are excellent examples of the diversity of the Carolinas style. Pink was born in Laurens, South Carolina, south of Spartanburg, on February 12, 1900, but for many years he lived in the quiet black section of Spartanburg. You had to walk up the steps to his house, and if he saw you coming he usually had time to get out to the porch to say hello before you got to the door. He was a tall, gangling man with an easy personality and a skilled, relaxed musical style. He thought of himself more as an entertainer than a bluesman and, when I recorded a three-album cross section of his music early in the sixties, the songs he did for the blues album were well-known, standard pieces; the only thing really personal about them was his own warmth and his skill with the guitar. Most of Pink's life was spent entertaining with little medicine shows or at tobacco or stock auctions. He was away from Spartanburg every year, traveling from town to town with whatever show had hired him for the season. He and a friend named Simmie Dooley worked for years with Doctor Kerr's show, and they recorded together for Columbia in Atlanta on April 14, 1928. The pieces they did, "Every Day in the Week Blues," "C.C. and O Blues," "Papa's 'Bout to Get Mad," and "Gonna Tip Out Tonight," were certainly chosen by Frank Walker to emphasize the blues part of their repertoire, but the singing was in the entertainment style of the shows, with the two of them alternating verses and harmonizing on choruses. The recordings were a glimpse into the world of the Piedmont medicine show. After Simmie's death Pink worked for many years with a one-legged harmonica player named Arthur Jackson, or "Peg Pete," who always seemed to be on the road when I tried to locate him in the early sixties. Pink had to stop traveling because of his health by 1961, and he suffered a stroke in 1964, ending his playing career.

Carl Martin was only peripherally associated with the Piedmont scene, but he certainly was an excellent guitarist in the Carolina style, and he was familiar with the local repertoire. He was from Virginia, Big Stone Gap, where he was born in 1906, and he moved to Knoxville, Tennessee, in the center of the Appalachians, when he was a teenager. Brownie McGhee was also from Knoxville and they must have known each other when they were both playing in the small city. Unlike Pink Anderson, Martin is a bluesman, with a busy, insistent guitar style based on the kind of ragtime technique that was prevalent in the twenties. He recorded at a number of sessions in Chicago in the mid-thirties. He'd moved there from Tennessee in 1932. Much of what he did was in a more Chicago-oriented style, but he could also record pieces like his "Old Time Blues" and "Crow Jane" that he did for Bluebird on July 27, 1935. He was associated with musicians like Bill Broonzy and Tampa Red during most of this period, but he still had kept his roots in the coastal style.

Of all the coastal bluesmen, however, the best known certainly was Paramount's recording artist Blind Blake. He was one of the most brilliant guitarists to record in the twenties as well as a strong, workmanlike singer and composer. His style was a shaping force in the new blues developing in the Carolinas, even though he wasn't part of the local musical scene, and still is one of the most elusive figures of the early blues.

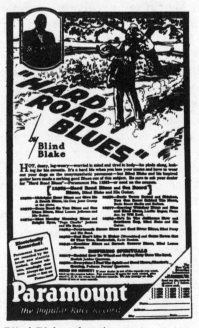

Blind Blake advertisement.

16.
Blind Blake

In a way it's misleading to include Blake in a discussion of the coastal school of blues, since he did all his recording in Chicago and was closely associated with the music scene there, but his style seems to be characteristic of a whole way of playing that developed in the southeastern states, and he was clearly an influence on the musicians there. Like the bluesmen from Virginia, he's part of a regional style while still uniquely separate from it. There's still no way, however, to tell how or where his style was formed, since he is one of the handful of major early bluesmen about whom almost nothing is known. In a way it's difficult to believe that so little is known about him, despite years of patient research. There was even some conjecture over his name, since some of the composer credits for his recordings list the name Arthur Phelps, which sometimes indicates the artist's real name when he's recording under a pseudonym. In a song he did with Papa Charlie Jackson, however, he clearly says that his name is Arthur Blake.

It's especially difficult to understand how Blake could have stayed so elusive. He wasn't an obscure artist with one or two records done by one of the itinerant field units. He was one of the major artists of the twenties, and all of his recording was done for Paramount, one of the leading blues labels. Between 1926 and 1931 or 1932 he recorded more than eighty titles and worked with musicians as well known as Johnny Dodds and Jimmy Bertrand. The Paramount publicity department distributed a photo and he was included in their advertising promotion, *The Paramount Book of the Blues*. But despite all this, what little we know of his life is fragmentary and incomplete. *The Paramount Book of the Blues* said only, by way of biography:

> . . . *Born in Jacksonville, in sunny Florida, he seems to have absorbed some of the sunny Florida atmosphere—disregarding the fact that nature had cruelly denied him a vision of outer things. He could not*

see the things that others saw—but he had a better gift. A gift of inner vision that allowed him to see things more beautiful. The pictures that he alone could see made him long to express them in some way—so he turned to music. He studied long and earnestly—listening to talented pianists and guitar players, and began to gradually draw out harmonious tunes to fit every mood. Now that he is recording exclusively for Paramount, the public has the benefit of his talent, and agrees, as one body, that he has an unexplainable gift of making one laugh or cry as he feels, and sweet chords and tones that come from his talking guitar express a feeling of his mood.

One musician who certainly knew Blake was Gus Cannon—he worked with him in Chicago, when Cannon recorded for Paramount as Banjo Joe. When I met Cannon in 1956 he still shook his head and smiled when he remembered Blake.

We drank so much whiskey! I'm telling you we drank more whiskey than a shop! And that boy would take me out with him at night and get me so turned around I'd be lost if I left his side. He could see more with his blind eyes than I with my two good ones.

What little that's known of Blake comes from these years in Chicago, though a relative in Patterson, Georgia, says that he came from Tampa and played in the southern Georgia-northern Florida area. In Chicago he lived at 4005 S. Parkway, where his landlady, Mrs. Renett Pounds, tried to look after him as best she could, despite his heavy drinking. In 1929 the *Chicago Defender* reported that he'd gotten in touch with a friend, George Williams, who was managing one of the touring road shows called the "Happy-Go-Lucky" show, and he toured with them until late 1930 or 1931, when he may have gone back to Jacksonville.

As difficult as it is to understand how there could be so little known about him, it's in a way as difficult to understand his popularity. He was a brilliant guitarist, but only an ordinary singer, and his songs had no clear textual identity. He seems to have had two important advantages, one that he was so early on the male blues scene, the other that he could turn out an almost indefinite number of reasonably proficient blues lyrics whenever a session was scheduled. Like every important blues company, Paramount had to have a steady stream of records with the favorite artists recording new material every few months, so that there could be regular new releases. Blake, and the other steady Paramount male blues artist, Blind Lemon Jefferson, were in and out of the studio, recording session after session, and both of them were popular for as long as they continued to record.

Even though Blake was recorded rather early in the rush to country blues, his voice is still disconcerting. He had a careful, clearly enuciated style that had some of the flavor of the vaudeville stage. In a line like

There's one thing in the world I can not understand

the "can" and "not" are carefully articulated, in a manner that would have been awkward for someone like Blind Lemon and, to an extent, sounded awkward for Blake. On an occasional piece like "Blake's Worried Blues" the singing is a little more impassioned, and there's a suggestion of Blind Lemon's vocal style in some of the phrasing, but most of his blues are reminiscent of the stage blues recorded by revue artists like Mamie Smith, Rosa Henderson, and Sarah Martin. On pieces like "Stonewall Street Blues" he even breaks into the double-time "jazzy" effect that Mamie Smith's back-up group, Johnny Dunn and His Jazz Hounds, used to throw in, and he sings one verse over stop chords in the guitar in the early jazz style. For one of his blues, "Goodbye Mama Moan," he used a Charleston dance beat throughout. His harmonic structuring also showed the effects of the vaudeville stage more than it did the back country. His first recording, "Early Morning Blues," made sometime in the early fall of 1926, is a twelve-bar blues, but the harmonic form is rather sophisticated, using a I to VI progression at the end of the repeated line, before going to the resolution in the final line. The complete verse is:

$$I - IV - I/IV - I7$$
$$IV - IV - I/IV - I/VI$$
$$II - V - I/IV - I$$

The singing stays closely within the bounds of the form. He's one of the few successful artists who never took any liberties with the twelve-bar form; this takes a measure of excitement and drama away from his performance, since there isn't a sense of any emotional force shaping the style. He continued to stay close to the harmonic patterns he set up with "Early Morning Blues" and used the same accompaniment figures in most of his blues. The melodies were also the same for many of his blues and almost any verse can be taken as typical of his melodic style.

*Raise note slightly in pitch (but not enough for it to become an *e*).

145

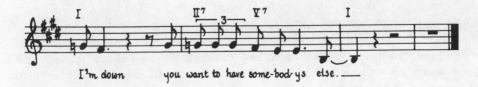

I'm down   you want to have some-bod-ys else. ___

The texts he assembled were effective, though lacking any strong individual quality. He used familiar verses, and the emotional situations he described were typical of the blues of this period:

> I'm worried now, I won't be worried long,
> I'm worried now, I won't be worried long.
> Brown I loved makes me sing this song . . .

or

> I'm goin' grab me a freight train, ride until it stops,
> I'm goin' grab me a freight train, ride until it stops.
> I ain't goin' stay around here and be your stumbling block. . . .

The uncertainties and instabilities of relationships with women were the continuing concern, and in the blues of the twenties the masculine role is almost completely passive, which could certainly be a reflection of the place in American society that the black man found himself, expressed as an almost helpless dependence on women and their emotional inconsistency. If there was an assertive text it was almost always specifically sexual, as in a song like "Hard Pushing Papa." This attitude was to change in the thirties, the newer blues perhaps in a way reflecting the beginning of a change in the way black men viewed themselves in the society. Blind Boy Fuller and Peetie Wheatstraw, who typify many of the new attitudes, both used many of the sexual boasts in their texts, but there was an overtone of self-confidence in what they were saying, even if often the texts included familiar verses. Blake, however, was still involved with the earlier concerns.

> Walkin', walkin', talkin' to myself,
> Walkin', walkin', talkin' to myself.
> Wonderin' if I die would my baby love somebody else.

A line from "Cold Love Blues" seems to express his feelings about the situation:

> Every day she treats me worser than the day before.

He usually was able to shape his material into a coherent statement, but the lack of originality often left a flatness to the complete text, and he sometimes borrowed verses from the vaudeville blues without bothering to make any changes, even if there were incongruities. One blues was clearly taken from a blues duet similar to the kind of songs that man and woman teams like Butterbeans and Susie, among others, were performing, but Blake sang it without seeming to notice that it was written as a dialog, especially in a verse like:

Tell me pretty Mama, where did you stay last night?
Tell me pretty Mama, where did you stay last night?
Ain't none of your business, daddy, since I treat you right.

Most of the bluesmen who used a verse with this construction usually added a "She said . . ." or a "She told me . . . " at the beginning of the final line to clarify the speaker.

But it's the other side of Blake's abilities—his guitar playing—that gives him his place in the development of the twenties blues style, and one of his best known solo pieces, "Southern Rag," also sheds some light on his own background. The solo was recorded sometime in October 1927, shortly after he did six blues earlier in the month. "Southern Rag," released on Paramount 12565, was the only piece he did at this session. The record begins with a brilliant display of what has come to be called "ragtime" guitar style—an alternating thumb bass, with a series of rhythmic clusters on changing chord harmonies. With decisive showmanship Blake delays some of the beats, anticipates others, catching a whole feeling of loose country dance and floating afternoon sunlight. Then he begins a spoken commentary that shifts suddenly into the coastal dialect of the Geechee and Gullah peoples of Georgia—a shift so easily done that it raises some question about Blake's background. Could he have spent some time on the Georgia sea islands? Perhaps he could even have some family background there—or was raised there himself—and Jacksonville, in northern Florida, was the city he'd come from last when Paramount asked him for some information. The accent is a hard one to imitate, but he seems so natural with it that it could be that it's his other accent that's not natural to him; that would explain the stiffness of his other singing on some records.

The great early black vaudevillian, Bert Williams, was a West Indian, and he had a similar problem with his speech pattern. His own English had a lilting West Indian accent, and he had to painfully learn an acceptable black "dialect" before he could successfully perform on the stage.

Blake's commentary begins in his usual accent:

Now we're (doin') an old Southern Rag. Way out there in all that cotton fields, where them people plant all that rice, make sugar cane, and peas and so forth grow.

Then he shifts into a Sea Island accent:

"Hey mawn, I want a match so you can light my pipe, yeah."
"Go on, old Geechee, I ain't studyin' 'bout ya."
"No, I know you ain't studyin' me now. Soon's you get my rice though I bet you study me then. Fancy you that."
"(Let's get) back in the row now. I should help pick this cotton or dig potato either one."

"I strip more rows of sugar cane than you strip in ten years!" Now we goin' do the dawnce now they call the Geechee dawnce. I goin' give you some music they call the Geechee music now.

The music he plays as Geechee music is a more freely rhythmed guitar picking, with less emphasis on the thumb stroke and a flowing arpeggiation in the upper strings. The Geechee people were felt to have retained more of the old African traditions, and playing in this manner is closer to the style of the older African instrumental music, particularly the playing of the kora. After the instrumental break he lapses back into the usual speech of his other recordings.

The rhythmic pattern for Blake's syncopated figures was not complex—usually a short sequence repeated on different chords. His own personal characteristic, however, was a double beat with his thumb, which he did by pulling the thumb over one string to make it sound, then hitting the next string with the thumb with the same continuous stroke. This gave the whole rhythmic figure a bouncing kind of anticipation, and his playing had an infectious lilt that was effective with everything from duets with Gus Cannon to his jazz recordings with Johnny Dodds.

He could also play a less restricted, more lyric style, and on at least one of his recordings—"Blake's Worried Blues," made at his first session in September 1926 and released on Paramount 12442—he played a solo chorus that was very similar in style to the guitar instrumentals on the records of Lonnie Johnson, who had started recording for OKeh ten months before. The solo is open and melodic, with a complete mastery of the instrument. There was this same sense of complete assurance in the three instrumentals he recorded in April 1928 with Dodds and Bertrand. Dodds, at this point, was one of the best known jazz musicians in Chicago. He was no longer recording with Louis Armstrong, with whom he'd done the immortal series of Hot Five and Hot Seven recordings between 1925 and 1927. Now he was recording with every important jazz name in the Chicago area, he was recording with his own orchestra, and he was leading a very successful band at the popular club "Kelly's Stables." Bertrand wasn't as well known as Dodds, but he was very active in Chicago, and in that city, at least, his reputation was as high.

In their trio session Blake more than holds his own. The three sides, "C. C. Pill Blues," "Hot Potatoes," and "South Bound Rag," were early collectors' items, not only for Dodds' presence, but because of the raw inventiveness and sheer drive of Blake's playing. Bertrand was a fine drummer and had recorded extensively playing the washboard, but for some reason Paramount had him play mostly slide whistle, with some wood blocks thrown in; so the entire rhythm was Blake's guitar. There was no feeling of rhythmic weakness. Blake was playing his alternating thumb style, with syncopated figures in the upper strings that he used as a contrast to Dodds' flowing, songlike style. Dodds seemed to feel completely free playing against his rock steady pulse, and it's the contrast between them, each playing at his best, that makes the records so memorable.

Some of Blake's recordings were released on Paramount's cheaper Broadway series during this period—though not the trio sides with Dodds. For these releases Paramount used the name Blind George Martin. Blake recorded steadily through the last years of the twenties, following a rough schedule of between six and ten songs in the spring—April or May—and another eight or ten in the fall—October or November. At his solo sessions he usually did several songs in one sitting. There was also a session with cornet and piano, and Jimmy Bertrand again, playing xylophone this time, in September or October 1928, when he did nine songs at once. After the trio sides with Dodds and Bertrand, Paramount used a number of other musicians with him for other releases, including a marvelous "Hastings Street Boogie" that he did with the Detroit pianist Charlie Spand at a session on August 17, 1929.

Despite the Depression, Blake went on recording, and he lasted longer than many other artists. There is some uncertainty about his final session, but he was still recording in 1932. His last recordings were released on the Paramount 13000 series, the last things pressed before the company slid into bankruptcy.

In the publicity portrait of him that Paramount sent out—the only photograph known of Blake—he looks thin and tall, long-legged and gangling. His eyes are closed, but he is smiling broadly, and his face has an open, broad warmth in its expression, as if he were pleased that someone was listening to him. As in the photograph of Blind Lemon that Paramount also sent out—which is the only known photo of him as well—Blake is dressed in a suit, his hair carefully trimmed, and the picture is taken against a bland studio background. Someone—probably an employee in the Paramount office—signed both photos "Cordially Yours" with a flowing signature. The picture, the recordings, and some hazy recollections are what we have of Blake as a person, but the bright, raggedy optimism of his guitar style was to change and develop in the hands of Carolina guitarists like Buddy Moss, so that what we have of his music is still a broad, echoing expression.

17.
Buddy Moss

Cultural history is no kinder than any other kind of history, and there's no assurance that the names or descriptions of a musical style have any more reality than the names describing an historical epoch. Of all the blues styles, only one is associated with a single individual—the Carolinas school of guitar playing that's usually called Blind Boy Fuller style. Certainly calling it that gives Fuller his full measure as a commercial artist—he was the best selling of all the East Coast bluesmen—but it's hard on people like Buddy Moss and Gary Davis, who played a significant role in the development of the style and who sometimes— Moss especially—found themselves described as Fuller imitators. Moss not only was in at the beginning, he recorded earlier as well, and some of the performances that were described as "in the style of Blind Boy Fuller" were recorded long before Fuller even got into a recording studio! Moss is an angry, resentful man now, and there's considerable reason for him to be disappointed at the assessment that was made of his music and his career.

Moss, fortunately, has been found in Atlanta and is still playing as well as ever, though he has had little success beginning a new career. In recent years he's been interviewed by a number of people, among them Bruce Bastin, who talked with him in connection with his excellent study of the Southeast blues styles, *Crying for the Carolinas*. There has been some recording, but a session he did for Columbia has never been released, and the other tapes made of him in performance have circulated among other record companies without success. Only a concert recording from the mid-sixties has been released, on Arnold Caplin's Biograph label. Moss is as brilliant as ever on it, but he is still living in semi-obscurity in Atlanta, playing for occasional festivals or for small blues clubs. If he were living in New York, where there is a denser gathering of blues enthusiasts with access to magazines and record companies, Moss probably would have had more of a chance, but he's decided to stay in Atlanta, where he's lived for much of his life.

It was circumstances, more than anything else, that curtailed Moss's career. From the beginning he was part of the commercial blues world. He was born in Jewell, Georgia, on January 26, 1914, his full name Eugene Moss. Jewell is north of Atlanta, in the northern Georgia clay hill country. He was there only until he was four, when his family moved to Augusta, on the South Carolina border not far from Statesboro, Georgia, where Willie McTell grew up. When he came to Atlanta he was still a teen-ager, but he was already a strong harmonica player, and he was part of the crowd that hung out along Decatur Street, which included McTell and the Hick brothers. His first recordings were made in the summer of 1930—July and August—when he did four numbers with Curley Weaver and Fred McMullen as the Georgia Cotton Pickers. The sessions were done for Frank Walker of Columbia Records and were released on the 14000 race series. Buddy was sixteen and Weaver was only twenty-four.

At the same time Buddy was learning the guitar—he remembers getting some lessons from Barbecue Bob Hicks and listening to records by Blind Blake and Blind Lemon. He certainly listened to Blind Blake's work, as did most of the other Georgia and Carolina musicians. It was Blake who was to be the strongest influence on their own style. Buddy probably also learned from Weaver, since they were close friends and Weaver had been playing the guitar for three or four years when they met. Moss became a much better guitarist than Weaver, but both of them had the same basic style of fingerpicking.

The early years of the Depression drifted over Atlanta, and the level of recording activity dropped. McTell had occasional sessions, but most of the other Atlanta men were silent. However, when recording began to pick up, Moss began with A.R.C. The first session was in New York on January 16, 1933, ten days before his nineteenth birthday. It was a loose Atlanta session, and he was back in the studio the next three days as well, recording eleven blues of his own and also playing with Fred McMullen, Curley Weaver, and Ruth Willis, who had come up to record at the same time. His first three songs had only his own guitar for accompaniment, "Bye-Bye Blues," "Daddy Don't Care," and "Red River Blues." For the other songs there was usually a second guitarist, who was either McMullen or Weaver, though he finished the final session playing alone. In his discussion of Moss's first sessions, Bruce Bastin has pointed out that there are even close similarities between these first pieces and later recordings of Fuller's. "Daddy Don't Care" seems to have been the direct source of Fuller's later "You've Got Something There," and there are similarities in the two guitar styles at many points. Moss never developed texts that were distinctly his own, but he had a strong sense of image, and often the force of the language overcame the awkwardness of occasional verses. In a blues beginning

> Walkin' down the hard road done wore the soles off my shoes,
> Walkin' down the hard road done wore the soles off my shoes,
> My soles are ragged, I got those hard road blues . . .

the vocal rhythms are uneven, and the verses he ties to it are overfamiliar; but there is a vividness to the opening image, and, since he manages to refer again to the hard road, the blues does have an emotional effect. The image lingers through the rest of the performance, even with the limp repeated rhyme of the final verse.

> Have you ever laid down at night, thinkin' about your brown?
> Have you ever laid down at night, thinkin' about your brown?
> And get the hard road blues and ramble from town to town.
>
> Reason why I start, why I low down,
> My gal done quit me, I got to leave this town.
> I put some wheels on my boogyin' shoes,
> Goin' to roll back to my baby to get rid of these hard road blues.
>
> I lay down last night, a thousand things on my mind,
> I lay down last night, a thousand things on my mind.
> Goin' to walk down these hard roads, just to cure my low down mind.

But even with the ordinariness of his texts, Moss was an effective artist. His voice was warm and responsive, without the swaggering roughness of Fuller's on the loose swinging pieces that Fuller did later, but with some of the close, personal appeal of Brownie McGhee, who was later a close friend of Moss's. All of the men from the area were influenced by the Blind Blake techniques, but Moss was one of the first to be able to play the complex instrumental flourishes Blake used. Moss had the same double thumb roll, and he used the clustered rhythms that Blake used.

The blues that Moss did were released by A.R.C. on their cheapest labels—the Banner, Melotone, Oriole, Perfect, and Romeo labels—as well as on the better known Vocalion label. The cheaper labels all sold for twenty-five cents apiece, and each line was labeled for a different retail chain. Romeo material, for example, could only be bought at S.H. Kress stores, and each of the others had their own store identity. This kind of distribution was one of the factors that kept Moss's name from collectors. The pressings were done on the poorest quality shellac, and there seems to have been only enough pressing to fill immediate orders. It was the height of the Depression, and sales of everything were small. The Vocalion releases were usually under the name of Jim Miller, but he and Weaver and McMullen also did some trio pieces that were released under the name Georgia Browns.

Despite all the difficulties of beginning a recording career in 1933, Buddy's releases seem to have sold. He was back in New York to record again nine months later—and this time there were five sessions between September 14 and 21. Weaver was with him again, but this time the third guitarist was Willie McTell, and as with the first session it's sometimes difficult to tell who's playing the second guitar. In one group of matrixes McTell is the singer for numbers 14045 to 14051, Moss sings on matrixes 14052 to 14054, Weaver then sings for the next four, and Moss sings "B & O Blues No. 2" and "Some Lonesome Day" on matrixes 14064 and 14065. The sessions were so informal that it's difficult to sort out which of them was playing. The next matrix is McTell singing "B & O Blues No. 2." The long day's work ended with Moss singing five more of his own pieces. What A.R.C. was recording was clearly intended to be a reasonably consistent group of pieces that they could merchandize steadily in the dime store outlets. In four days of recording the three of them did forty-four sides—which not only means a lot of hard work, but also drains away any material they might have to use. It wasn't surprising that before the end of it they were singing each other's songs and that it's sometimes a little difficult to tell who is playing guitar.

A.R.C. continued recording Buddy; he had that ability, necessary in the thirties, of being able to come up with an unending stream of songs which, though they weren't markedly original as far as their texts went, were consistently musical, and he played with his usual technical brilliance. In 1934 and 1935 he recorded thirty-five blues, enough to keep the stores in new releases on a regular schedule. But after the last session on August 28, 1935, his career virtually ended. At this time he was living in Greensboro, Georgia, and he went to jail there, dropping out of the musical scene for six years

Bruce Bastin also interviewed the white businessman J.B. Long, who was managing Blind Boy Fuller and other artists during this period, and Bastin described what happened to Moss in the late thirties in his book *Crying for the Carolinas*.

> . . . *His successful recording career was terminated, although he was finally permitted to work as janitor at the County Courthouse in Greensboro, a post given to trustees there. Art Satherley of ARC wrote to Moss requesting that he write to J.B. Long, to see if he could get him out on parole. Long drove down to see the parole board and put a strong case for Moss's release on parole. Long was willing to offer Moss a job on a 70-acre farm that he had near Burlington and give him $30 a week plus rent and board—no mean sum in those days. At this time, Long was mayor of Elon, where he still lives, and the local chief of police lived only three doors away! On top of this, he could promise that Moss would get a further recording session with ARC; and he would be living out of Georgia anyway. Although that particular parole board was soon discharged for selling pardons, Long put his case to the new board and parole was granted. Moss travelled to stay with Long in Elon, working two or three days a week at Long's home and in the store at weekends. It was here that he got to know Brownie McGhee—with whom he is still in touch—as well as the Trice brothers. He did in fact record again for OKeh in 1941, using Sonny Terry and Red to accompany him, while on some tracks Brownie McGhee played piano, for example Joy Rag. However, the war and the resultant economic and union restrictions on the recording industry meant that Moss dropped out of sight until his re-discovery in Atlanta in the mid-'60s.*

The years that he spent working for Long also meant the end of his reputation as a bluesman. Fuller began recording for A.R.C. a month before Moss's last sessions, and he became immediately popular. His records sold well, and they sold in larger and larger numbers as the economy began to drag itself out of the worst of the Depression. The pressing quality improved, the distribution widened, and Fuller's records were sold by the thousands. This doesn't mean that Fuller didn't deserve his success. He had an ability to project himself and his whims and his excitements and his unhappiness that Moss had never had, even at his best. But Fuller's style was certainly the same style that Moss had begun recording years earlier. The reason collectors called Moss a Fuller imitator was that they found Fuller's records first. There were more of them, and they came much later than Moss's. Fuller records were among the first blues records you found when you junked for old blues records in the South. Moss's turned up later—they weren't so well recorded, and they were usually worn. It was easy to categorize him as a Fuller imitator.

It's hard to see, after so many years, why Moss wasn't recorded again while he was working on Long's farm, especially since it was A.R.C.'s recording director who had asked him to write to Long. It might have been that the terms of Moss's parole didn't leave him free to travel as far as New York—but probably it was the success of Fuller that kept him doing his odd jobs. Fuller had become so well established for A.R.C.—selling mostly on the higher-priced Vocalion label— that Satherley didn't need Moss, especially with a style that was so similar. Perhaps Decca could have used Moss for their blues series, but as long as Long was managing Fuller there doesn't seem to have been a chance for Moss. He didn't record again, in fact, until after Fuller's death, and after his enforced silence he didn't sound as individual as he had six years earlier.

Moss, today, is still resentful over what happened to him, a chunky, dark-skinned man, with an intense expression, still a brilliant guitarist and musician, and almost restlessly looking for a chance to get back some of the success he had in his early years. At least he's no longer considered simply one of the many followers of Blind Boy Fuller—but there's still been no major reevaluation of his importance in the development of the Carolina blues style.

18.
Blind Boy Fuller and Blind Gary Davis

When you come into Durham, North Carolina, on back roads—in from the rolling, flat countryside around the small city—you get the feeling that most of it must be warehouses. The long, windowless shapes of the tobacco warehouses line the back streets. Durham has other sections—it's as modern a city now as you can find in North Carolina—but there is always that lingering impression of those rows of warehouses. Tobacco has always dominated North Carolina's economy, from its first years as an English colony, and it still is a tobacco town, with the countryside around divided into the careful fields that are characteristic of tobacco culture. With the tobacco there were jobs and money, and that meant that Durham swelled in the first decades of the 1900s—growing at the expense of the surrounding farm country. It meant a growing black population with some income, but still close to the country roots of their own culture. It also meant—since one comes on the heels of the other—bluesmen, drawn to the city's streets and taverns, struggling to make a living from the country people still hungry for the blues.

The streets of Durham—and the other cities of the North Carolina tobacco country, like Winston-Salem or Rocky Mount—are silent now. Only passing traffic, people lounging in open doors on hot summer afternoons, children playing along the street—the bluesmen who used to sing along Durham's streets have been gone now for long years. But, as the Durham musician and writer Bill Phillips described in a spring 1974 article in the Atlanta publication *Southern Exposure:*

> In 1935, if one were to travel one block south from Main Street in Durham, across the railroad tracks, one would see the proud store fronts and bustling enterprises of Durham's black business section. The black middle class was pushing for whatever heights were attainable in a segregated society. The Biltmore Hotel played host to the

likes of Cab Calloway, Count Basie, and Bessie Smith. A few doors down, the Bull City Barber Shop catered to the vanities of fashionable folk, and the Carolina Times *in the next block chronicled the passing events.*

This is where the action was—and where Blind Boy Fuller and friends could be found. Possibly Gary Davis just walked around the corner eluding his social worker (always curious if Davis made money on the streets) and taking some time off between his frequent visits at church meetings. Street singing during this time was an art practised throughout the South by urban blues singers. Although nobody got rich at it, a surprising amount of money could be made by a talented musician. Since the city viewed it as begging, a letter sanctioning the activity was periodically sent from a welfare official to the police chief. For example:

April 8, 1933

Mr. G.W. Proctor   In re: Fulton Allen (Col.)
Chief of Police   606 Cameron Avenue
Durham, N.C.   City

Dear Mr. Proctor:
    If it meets with your approval we are glad to recommend that the above named man be allowed to make music on the streets of Durham at a place designated by you.
    Assuring you that we are always glad to cooperate with you, I am

Your very truly

W.E. Stanley
Supt. Public Welfare

The Fulton Allen referred to in the letter was, of course, better known as Blind Boy Fuller, and he eked out a living in Durham by singing on the streets, with a relief check of $23 a month, and with the income he earned, from 1935 to 1940, as a prolific and successful recording artist. He felt completely at ease playing in the streets. Another Durham musician, Willie Trice, talking to Bruce Bastin, remembered Fuller playing on the New York streets in 1937:

On the day following their arrival in New York to record for Decca, Willie Trice remembers being woken about 11 a.m. by Fuller, already neatly and smartly dressed as always. He never wore dark glasses or shades and his cap was always on his head; he never went bare-headed nor wore a hat. Fuller was impatient to get out on the New York streets—by no means unfamiliar to him by this time—and he dragged Willie out of bed to take him down, where he played for about an hour before coming back into the hotel.

It's difficult to tell with any exactness when they all got to Durham. The letter asking the police to let Fuller sing on the streets of Durham is useful, because it makes it clear that he was there at least before April 1933. In the late thirties there seem to have been days when Fuller, Gary Davis, and Sonny Terry—the great Carolinas harmonica player who was also blind—played together along Pettigrew Street, or close to the tobacco warehouse gates when the workers were getting off. These moments must have been some of the most electrifying that could be found in the blues in the thirties. Fuller with his solid, steady rhythm and brilliant picking, Gary Davis with his startling runs and complex rhythmic variety, and Sonny with his "whooping" harmonica style. Fuller usually worked on the street with his washboard player, Oh Red (George Washington), so he would have been there as well, adding his percussive, rushing beat to all of it. If they didn't make a good living at it, it was only because times were hard, and the men coming out of the factory gates in their sweat-dark shirts and sagging overalls didn't have much money either.

But this was the late thirties, and it had been a period of years before they got to know each other and started playing together in Durham. Davis seems to have moved into the city about 1935—he's listed in the city directory for the first time that year—though he might have been there even earlier. Sonny Terry might have come in about the same time, though he probably met Fuller the year before and stayed at Fuller's house when he first came to Durham, so it could have been in 1934. Davis was considerably older than the other two—39—and Fuller was in his mid-twenties, a year or two older than Sonny.

Of the Durham musicians—and of all the guitar players and singers in the Carolinas—the dominant musician among them probably was Gary Davis. It wasn't only that he was older and that he'd had a longer involvement with the kind of East Coast finger style that Blind Blake represented. Gary Davis is one of the great blues performers—even if he stopped playing the blues at an early stage. There are only two blues recorded by him in the thirties—as part of a session he did with Fuller when he also recorded a group of gospel songs—but they are uniquely brilliant. They represent a fusion of a localized style—the Southeast guitar ragtime technique—with the individual genius of a great performer. It isn't a style that would be popular with a general blues audience. It's too startling, too sudden in its changes and inflections, too free in its technical flashes—as he lets himself respond freely to the implications of his material. There's no sign that his two sides ever made any impression on the thirties record buyer, any more than the recordings of Skip James, the Mississippi singer who seems most like him in a kind of personal genius, made an impression—but Gary was a guitar player's guitar player, and his influence can be heard on the whole body of Carolinas music recorded in the thirties. His influence in later years—on New York's young folk guitarists—was so pervasive that his style finally became one of the world's most widespread guitar sounds. It wasn't his own recordings that were so popular but the recordings of people influenced by him, from Blind Boy Fuller to a whole generation of New York City folk singers; these continue to reach an audience that is worldwide.

This is clear not only from the testimony of older musicians who remember Davis's startling brilliance but from the records themselves. Much of what he did is also there on the recordings that were made after he came onto the scene. Only Buddy Moss is also mentioned as one of the root sources of the style that finally developed, and he is never described as the guitarist Davis was. Instead he's talked about as an early influence, someone who got into it first, and who was a fine performer—while Davis was something unique. As Willie Trice, a younger Durham musician who knew and played with them all, told Bill Phillips: "While you were playing one chord, Gary would play five."

Davis, a short, stocky, rumpled man when he was later part of the New York folk scene, has talked often about his early life, but some details are still vague, and he has always refused to discuss the circumstances of his blindness. It certainly isn't because he doesn't remember what happened to him. I drove him around New York in one period, when we were working on a recording together, and he would talk about his childhood and things from the years when he was beginning as a musician. It was spring, and I often drove him up the East River Drive in New York to his shabby apartment in the Bronx. He liked the window open in the car; we could feel the warmth in the air, and it brought back memories of his life on the small farm where he'd grown up in Laurens County, South Carolina. He was born there in 1896, April 30, so he was remembering back almost sixty years as he talked. He could remember how his grandmother made new bread from the ends of the old dried corn cakes, and he could remember that the hilly farm country was so lonely " . . . you couldn't hear nothing but owls after sundown."

Like most of the musicians who became bluesmen, he started playing when he was still a child.

> The first time I ever heard a guitar played I thought it was a brass band coming through. I was a small kid and I asked my mother what was it and she said that was a guitar. I said, "Ain't you going to get me one of those when I get large enough?" She said, "Yeah, I'll get you one." First thing I learned to play was an old banjo, you understand, I say old banjo because I learned how to play that. I was just going up and down, plunk a lunk, plunk a lunk, plunk a lunk. I thought I was doing something, playing that banjo.

The blues also came early for him. He remembers that it was in 1911.

> The first song that was a blues I heard was a man in a carnival singing "I'm on the road somewhere, if the train don't break down I'm on the road somewhere." . . . Then "Memphis Blues" and "Florida Blues" and some girl blues, kind of imitate to her feeling. This come to be very famous . . .

Much of Davis's early life is vague, but about this time he seems to have moved into Greenville, a busy market town in the northwest corner of South Carolina. It isn't far from Spartanburg, and between the two cities there was a large group of guitarists and singers. Josh White was to become the best known of the Greenville musicians, but he began traveling as a lead boy with blind singers when he was very young—he was born in Greenville on February 11, 1914—and he wasn't part of the musical scene, even though he came back from time to time to see his mother. Gary was married while he was living in Greenville, and he was playing in a large string band. He seems to have been in Greenville for many years—until the late 1920s—and he only left when his wife moved in with another musician, also blind, named Joe Walker. By this time Gary had been blind for many years and was pretty well able to get around by himself. He had been playing with musicians of considerable ability. Willie Walker was one of the members of the string band, and Joe Walker, the man Gary's wife left him for, was remembered as a strong guitarist.

Sometime after he left Greenville he went through his religious conversion, and in 1933 he was ordained as a minister in Washington, North Carolina, a small town about ninety miles outside of Durham. He seems to have come into Durham not long after, and he immediately became close to Fuller, who had come into the city a year or two earlier. In his article on Durham's musicians, Bill Phillips described a little of their life during this period.

Through the Depression, both men depended on the Durham County Welfare Dpartment for periodic aid. And our few glimpses of their lives during this period come from the reports of their caseworkers. In order to be eligible for their $23 a month assistance, Fuller and Davis had to conceal the irregular income from their music, and the welfare records reveal a constant cat-and-mouse game with officials trying to determine their clients' eligibility. "Yes ma'am," Davis told an official who managed to find him in his rented room. "I know you been here several times, but you know I am inclined to preach the gospel, and I got to be gone a lot since God called me." The worker asked if he made any money on these trips. Davis wryly answered, "The only success I have is saving souls, which is pay enough." Before the caseworker could continue, Mary Hinton, Davis' kindly landlord, interrupted, complaining that the heat was about to kill her. That started Davis on a sermon about being prepared to die. Taking his text from "Be ye also ready," Davis launched into a detailed sermon on the necessity of preparation for the inevitable "flight to glory." He concluded by giving the worker a pamphlet he had written on the constancy of death, a theme which runs through many of Davis' songs. . . .

On another occasion, Mary Hinton elaborated on Davis' religious convictions. "His mind runs backwards, you know, and I believe it's because he has just thought about the Bible and religion too much. A person can think too much, and I believe Gary has. He sometimes

159

*wakes me up at two or three o'clock in the morning going to bed, fall-
ing over a chair. He sits up and reads his Bible that late.*

At some point when he was younger Gary had attended the South Carolina
Blind School and learned to read New York point, a kind of Braille, and his
requests to the welfare workers over the years often mentioned a new Bible.
It was also during these years that he was influencing the Durham musicians,
his guitar playing so impressing them that years later the Trice brothers still
shake their heads over his ability. Willie's final judgment was that Davis was
" . . . the playingest man I ever saw." Certainly he left an indelible impression
on the music of Blind Boy Fuller, and the style that grew in Durham's quiet
streets was to make a strong mark on the blues of the thirties.

Although Fuller has been dead since 1940, he has never been an elusive figure
in blues history. When I was gathering material for *The Country Blues* in the
late 1950s, Sonny Terry and Brownie McGhee were often in the old offices of
Folkways Records on West 46 Street in New York, and we'd talk about Fuller
when we were in the office at the same time. His widow, Cora, is still living in
Durham, and J.B. Long still has a store in Burlington, outside of Durham,
where Bruce Bastin talked with him. Fuller was born in Wadesboro, North Caro-
lina, a small town close to the border of South Carolina, about 1908 or 1909.
His father was Calvin Allen, his mother's name Mary Jane. Fulton, as he was
named at birth, was one of ten children. When he met the woman he was to
marry, Cora Mae Martin, in 1927, the family had moved to Rockingham. She
knew little about his earlier life, except that they hadn't been in Rockingham
long before she met him. He was already partially blind, though she didn't
know what had caused his sight problem. His eyesight was growing worse, and
he became completely blind a year and a half after they were married. He had
been playing a little music when they met, but when his sight failed he was
just twenty—or maybe still in his teens—and there was no way for him to do
any kind of work. He seems to have gotten help from local welfare agencies
from the beginning, but at the same time he turned more and more to music
as a way of making a living.

It's probable—as Bastin suggests—that Fuller came to music late enough so that
he was primarily influenced by the phonograph record and by musicians that
he met when he was playing. Also, by the late 1920s when he seems to have
started playing fairly regularly, there was a great deal of recorded blues, and the
forms and the styles were becoming rather clearly defined. If someone wanted
to become a professional musician there were a number of sources of material
for him and it wasn't necessary to synthesize a local style. Fuller listened to a
lot of records, by Blind Blake certainly, among others, and he learned from the
musicians around him. Some people remember him as easy to get along with, a
small, neatly dressed man who enjoyed playing and worked at his music. Willie
Trice, another Durham bluesman who knew Fuller well and went with him on
the 1937 trip to New York, told Bill Phillips that although Fuller was easy to
get along with, he also carried a pistol with him and had a "fiery" temper. "If

Fuller got mad at you, you better stand still and not say a word." He threatened to shoot J.B. Long during their disputes later in his career, and sometime in the thirties he did shoot his wife in the leg. Long was able to keep him out of jail, since Cora, as the only witness, wouldn't testify against him.

Fuller is usually remembered as wearing good clothes, always with a cap or hat on, difficult to get along with at times, but usually friendly. The group of musicians around him in Durham was close and mutually respectful in the way that the group around Bob Hicks was in Atlanta. He left Rockingham with Cora not long after they were married, and they first lived in Winston-Salem, another tobacco center west of Durham, in the low foothills of the Appalachians. They lived there on the streets close to the tobacco warehouses, also close to his brother Milton who was living in the city. They tried Danville, Virginia, for two months, another small city just over the North Carolina state line, then moved to Durham. He seems to have been in touch with the welfare authorities, since there was the letter from their office to the Durham police in 1933.

Fuller certainly wasn't the first of the Carolina musicians to record. Buddy Moss—from Georgia, but playing in a similar Blind Blake-derived style—had been recording since 1932, and Josh White—another Carolina bluesman who was to have a remarkable career as a folk and cabaret artist in New York later—had also started recording for the American Recording Corporation in 1932. It wasn't until three years later that Fuller got into a recording studio. J.B. Long finally heard him and took him to A.R.C. As Bastin described it:

> In 1935, Long was promoted to manager of the United Dollar Stores at 2501 W. Club Boulevard in Durham, where Fuller had been living on Beaumont or Murphy Street, just off the negro [sic] "black bottom" on East Pettigrew. Parallel to Pettigrew are the railroad tracks and across these are the tobacco factories and warehouses upon which Durham's wealth depends. It was inevitable that Long and Fuller should meet. Long had been informed of a blind singer/guitarist who played behind the warehouses for dimes and nickels. By this time, Long had been selling blues records for some years, especially remembering Josh White's Blood Red River/Pickin' Low Cotton and Buddy Moss numbers. He appreciated the demand for blues and knew them very well, as buyers would quote a line, or only a few words, and expect Long to know on which record they appeared. Thus, when Fuller was led to Long's store, Long was not surprised and one of the longest relationships between manager and artist in the blues of the '30s began.

Bastin didn't make clear that this was not only an extended relationship, it was almost a unique one. Usually the artists worked directly with the company, without any kind of business manager or agent to handle the business affairs for them. Long was not only a shrewd judge of talent; he had some idea of the kinds of money that could be made, and although he now says that it was more or less a hobby for him, the musicians who worked for him, such as Sonny Terry, felt that he treated them badly as far as the money was concerned. Sonny, talking about it in the Folkways office, was able to shrug it off.

Long got us recording, you know, and at the beginning he got all the money. We didn't care, 'cause it got us our start.

Fuller, however, seems to have resented the arrangement, threatened to shoot Long, and in 1937 made a strong effort to break loose and go his own way, but Long, who represented the very popular gospel quartet, Mitchell's Christian Singers, as well as Fuller, was too important for the companies to ignore, and the one session Fuller managed to do without Long was partly held off the market until after Fuller's death. Long was from a small North Carolina town, Hickory, and he'd been selling records in small general merchandise stores for several years when he began finding talent for the companies himself. He worked with both white and black artists, but he was considerably more successful with black music. The first sessions were done with the Mitchell Christian Singers in August 1934, and Fuller began recording in July 1935.

Long didn't go to New York with Fuller himself, but he sent him up as part of a Durham group. Another Durham singer, George Washington, who often led Fuller on the streets, seems to have taken care of getting Fuller there, and Gary Davis went along as well. Washington, who was often known as Bull City Red— the nickname coming from Durham's nickname of Bull City—usually played washboard with Fuller, but he also was an excellent guitarist in the Durham style, and he recorded at the same time. They were in the studio for four days, July 23, 24, 25 and 26, and the sessions were all productive. Fuller himself did twelve blues, Washington did eight, and Gary did his two blues as well as gospel material. For two of the numbers, "Rag, Mama, Rag" and "Baby You Gotta Change Your Mind," they played together as their old street trio, with Fuller and Davis on guitars and Washington playing washboard. The recording of "Rag, Mama, Rag," released on both A.R.C. and Vocalion labels with "I'm a Rattlesnakin' Daddy" on the other side, was rather successful, and Fuller's career was on its way.

Davis was the second guitarist on half of the songs Fuller did, and their accompaniment duets are often distinctively exciting. Davis's freer and more spontaneous playing seemed to give Fuller a sense of loose exuberance, and something like "Rag, Mama, Rag" moved with a carefree strut, like a boy laughing as he runs a stick along a picket fence. This kind of small blues group was to be very successful for Fuller over the five years he was to record. For the next session, however, in New York nine months later, April 28 and 29, 1936, he worked by himself. There were ten blues, two recorded the first day and eight the second. Probably at the request of Art Satherley, the A.R.C. recording director, when he came back to New York for his third group of sessions, in February 1937, he had Washington with him again, and another local guitarist, this time Floyd Council, usually known as Dipper Boy Council. They did fourteen blues, but Council played on only four of Fuller's titles. During the same session Council also did six blues of his own, finally released under the name "Blind Boy Fuller's Buddy" or "The Devil's Daddy-in-Law," as an answer to Peetie Wheatstraw, the St. Louis bluesman who had been recording since 1930 as "The Devil's Son-in-Law." The names were used as smaller titles under his own name on the record labels.

By this time, after less than two years of recording, Fuller had created an extensive body of blues, and he'd finally developed the style and the persona that carried him through the rest of his career. He found an image of himself that he could project on records, and it was in many ways a masculine counterpart of the themes that Memphis Minnie was developing in her recordings. There was a continuation of the old abject unhappiness at women's unfaithfulness or their demands, but, unlike singers of the twenties such as Blind Blake or Peg Leg Howell, Fuller often included verses of this type in blues that had much more assertive emotional attitudes. He could sing a verse like

> A working man ain't nothin' but a woman's slave,
> A working man nothin' but a woman's slave.
> When she start to lovin', Great God! it just won't 'have

which seems to be the more familiar twenties abject plea, but then in the same blues he went on:

> Have my dinner ready, don't let my coffee be cold,
> I said have my dinner ready, woman, don't let my coffee be cold.
> And don't forget, baby, save my sweet jelly roll

with a near swagger in his voice, telling his woman what he expected from her.

Also, like Memphis Minnie, Fuller used a self-projection that didn't really reflect the realities of his domestic situation. Minnie, who was married and living with a husband during most of her career, sang blues after blues about men leaving her and her response to the situation. Fuller, who is also remembered as living a generally quiet home life, sang blues after blues where at some point he emphasized his sexual proficiency.

> Said I got a new way of lovin' think it must be bad,
> I got a new way of lovin' think it must be bad.
> Said these here North Carolina women won't let Blind Boy Fuller rest.

In another blues he could say:

> I never loved, but a thousand women in my life,
> Oh no, a thousand women in my life.

In another:

> Hey mama, hey girl, don't you hear Blind Boy Fuller calling you.
> She's so sweet, so sweet,
> My little woman, so sweet.

This was all bound into a blues context of more or less familiar verses and attitudes, and the dominant mood was less assertive, more resigned, and there were many verses like:

> But I'm goin' find my little woman, don't think she can't be found.
> I say, hey hey, don't think she can't be found.
> I'm goin' walk this hard hard road 'till my moustache drag the ground.

But there was the other side, the sexual boaster, the strong, assertive male figure that became the persona of his blues, although the texture, the structure of his material stayed close to the conventional patterns of the late thirties blues song.

At the same time that he was developing and defining his style Fuller was also becoming very successful, so successful that he tried to break off his arrangement with Long. Long's name was on most of the compositions Fuller had done as "composer," and this, as well as his practice of keeping most of the recording fees his artists got, meant that he was making the money. Long told Bastin that he did write the pieces and used verses he'd heard on other blues or made up, so perhaps he did compose some of the songs Fuller performed but Long was certainly working in a black idiom, and there was nothing in his texts that differed significantly from what other musicians in the Durham area were doing; so it would seem Fuller should have gotten the copyrights for the songs. Certainly when Fuller did break away and record on his own, the song material was almost identical with the kind of thing he'd been recording before; the only difference was that this time it was his name on the label as composer.

It was Mayo Williams, working as recording director for Decca's 7000 race series, who got Fuller briefly away from Long's heavy paternalism. Willie Trice, another Durham musician who was close to Fuller, told Bastin that it was Fuller who contacted Mayo Williams and that Williams came down to Durham to talk with him. When Williams met him Fuller was with the Trice brothers, Willie and his brother Richard, and Fuller insisted that they go along as well. It was on this trip to New York in 1937 that Willie had to take Fuller down to the street so he could do a little playing before they went to the studio. Fuller did twelve blues, ten on July 12 and two more on July 14. The Trices got their chance on July 13, doing six sides, two as a duet, and one solo record each. Willie remembers it as a strained and difficult time. Fuller was to do twelve sides, but an electrical storm came up the first day before he could finish, and he had to postpone the last two songs. The Trices were nervous and unsure of themselves, and the studio was hot and confining. Neither they nor Mayo Williams was happy with the result. He didn't bring them into the studio again, and of the six sides they did, two of them—the duet—were never released, and Richard's record wasn't released until two years later.

Long was taken by surprise by the first release from the Decca sessions—"If You See My Pigmeat" and "Why Don't My Baby Write to Me?" on Decca 7877—and according to Bastin was able to stop the release of the rest of the session. However, subsequent releases follow in close numerical sequence—"You Never Can Tell" and "Bulldog Blues" were the next number, Decca 7878—and it seems that Decca simply spaced out what they had, since Williams realized he wasn't going to get Fuller into the studio again. Long, in fact, had Fuller in New York again less than two months later, on September 7, 8, and 9, and some of the material was done again. "Bulldog Blues" became "Bull Dog Blues" and "Put You Back in Jail" became "Throw Your Yas Yas Back in Jail."

Perhaps because he'd hurried Fuller back into the studio to protect his A.R.C. contract Long sent him by himself, but only three months later he sent him back to New York again, this time with still another Durham musician—one of the greatest Carolinas bluesmen, and one of the greatest blues harmonica players, Sonny Terry. It was such a successful partnership that they were to stay together until Fuller's death and some of the sides they made together—often with Bull City Red or Oh Red, as he was later called—were among the most exciting blues done in the late thirties. It is difficult to believe that Long could have found another fine musician in Durham, but Terry was drawn to the city because of Fuller, and the Durham area was becoming better and better known as a blues center.

To see Sonny Terry play now—to listen to his sudden rhythmic sweeps and intensely lyric melodic lines—makes it almost impossible to believe that he's been recording for nearly forty years. His playing still has all the fire and the intensity of someone making his first record, and he seems to hunch over the harmonica as though he still expects to find something new in it every time he plays. Like the other musicians he came from outside of Durham, and in 1959, when we talked about his career for *The Country Blues*, he said that it was Fuller who brought him in. In the mid-thirties, perhaps 1937, when Fuller was visiting his sister in Watha, North Carolina:

> ... *A harmonica player heard Fuller was in town, and went up to the house and asked if he could play some blues with him. They played together for three or four hours, and Fuller told him to look for him in Durham and they'd try to get a job together. The harmonica player was the young Sonny Terry.*

> *Sonny, like Fuller, was from North Carolina. He was born outside of Durham, October 24, 1911. He was born Sanford Terrell, the son of a farmer named Reuben Terrell. There were three brothers, Willie, Ronald, and Ashbury. He grew up on his father's twenty-acre farm learning to play the harmonica when he was still a little boy. His father was a good harmonica player and started Sonny on his favorite little songs, "Lost John" and "Fox Chase." A well-known harmonica player named DeFord Bailey came through town and Sonny learned a little from him, but mostly he picked it up from his father. When he was just learning, he'd sit for hours imitating the sounds of the trains that passed in the distance.*

165

*When Sonny met Fuller he was nearly blind himself. When he was
eleven, he was beating a stick against a chair and a piece of it broke
off and flew into his eye. The sight in that eye was impaired. Five
years later a boy threw a small piece of iron at Sonny and put out his
other eye. He realized that he'd have to start playing on the streets to
make a living; so he started going into Durham and Raleigh, playing
all afternoon; then walking home alone in the darkness. When he met
Fuller he was twenty-three, playing in a distinctive wailing style that
was a fine contrast to Fuller's dark voice.*

When Sonny moved to Durham he stayed with Fuller and his wife Cora and
their adopted daughter at 805 Colfax. They soon were playing together on Dur-
ham's streets and J.B. Long got them into the recording studio.

With Sonny and Oh Red accompanying him, Fuller soon was to become more
and more important as a recording artist. The country was beginning to shake
off some of the effects of the Depression; sales generally were increasing, and
Fuller was one of the artists who was part of the general swell. Also he had be-
come even more productive with Terry. They did ten sides on their first ses-
sions—December 15 and 16, 1937—then in 1938, in April and October, they
did twenty-two songs together. In 1938 there were fourteen Blind Boy Fuller
records released, more than any other blues artist. He was still getting very little
of the money he was earning, and he made another futile effort to get free of
Long, this time with the help of a caseworker from the State Blind Commission,
William Lewis. Bill Phillips was able to reconstruct some of what happened
from welfare reports and from Willie Trice's recollection.

*. . . Fuller resented Long's middle-man profits and on at least one re-
cording trip became so enraged he threatened to shoot him. "After a
lot of talking," Willie Trice recalled, "he finally cooled down." In
1939, Fuller hoped to get out from under Long's management alto-
gether and, since the State Blind Commission encouraged self-suffi-
cency, caseworker William Lewis began seeking an independent con-
tract with a record company for Fuller.*

*Lewis learned that Fuller was under contract to Long to receive $200
each time he recorded twelve songs, although that amount varied de-
pending on whose word is relied upon. Fuller and Lewis came to the
agreement that Fuller would not renew his current contract with
Long, which would expire on April 21, 1939,.and Lewis wrote both
Long and the American Recording Corporation explaining this
intent. Neither answered. Upon the expiration of the contract, Long
wrote Lewis saying that while Fuller was no longer under contract to
him, he was still bound to the American Recording Company. When
Lewis wrote A.R.C. they simply referred him back to Long. In the
wake of the confusion, Fuller agreed to go record for Long in Mem-
phis with Sonny Terry in July, 1939. So ended Fuller's efforts at
gaining an independent contract.*

The sessions in the summer of 1939 were particularly productive. On July 12 Fuller, Sonny Terry, and Oh Red did twelve blues. Some of them were covering successes by other artists, like Big Bill, and they did a "Jivin' Big Bill Blues," but others were continuing the persona of the hard swaggerer that Fuller had shaped in his earlier work. There were specific sexual cries like "I Crave My Pig Meat" and "I Want Some of Your Pie," and there was the strain of good-natured boasting that he'd begun in earlier blues like "I'm a Good Stem Winder" from the April 1938 session.

On the same day that they did their twelve blues, July 12, they stayed on and did three religious songs, the first that Fuller had recorded. They sang as a vocal trio and recorded "Have You Decided (Which Way to Go)?," "I See the Sign of Judgement," and "Everybody Wants to Know How I Die." The next day they did three more religious songs, "I Feel Like Shoutin'," "Jesus Touched Me," and "Talkin' with Jesus." There doesn't seem to have been any significance to this. Like most bluesmen Fuller also knew a lot of gospel songs, and religious material was selling well again. Art Satherley released the records under the name "Brother George and His Sanctified Singers," though they were clearly recognizable to anyone who was a regular buyer of Fuller's blues releases. It was still another instance of the old prejudice against bluesmen singing sacred songs. Josh White, also recording for Satherley, was "Pinewood Tom" on his blues releases and "Joshua White (The Singing Christian)" on his religious recordings.

Fuller's popularity continued to grow, and 1940 began as one of his biggest years. There were three sessions—again with Sonny Terry and Oh Red—in March, then another twelve-blues sessions on June 19. They were mixing sacred and blues material rather freely, and the songs ranged from the great hymn "Twelve Gates to the City" that Davis was to record several times later in New York, to a number of brilliant blues performances on songs like "I Don't Want No Skinny Woman" or "Thousand Woman Blues."

Sonny Terry had also started recording under his own name, and the three of them did a stunning "Harmonica Stomp" that's a classic example of country dance music on March 6; it was released on OKeh 05538. The day before there had been an unaccompanied harmonica solo and a startling harmonica and washboard duet—a loose, raggy stomp that had the headlong feel of a farm tractor wheeling down a dirt road. It was released on OKeh 05453 as "Harmonica and Washboard Breakdown."

Most of the material from the June session was released on the OKeh label, and it seems to have been aggressively distributed. Copies of the records were to be found in large quantities in junk shops and salvage stores everywhere in the South in the 1950s. These were some of Fuller's finest recordings—exciting and colorful and inventive, with an almost virtuoso brilliance in his rhythmic extensions and vocal lines. He seemed to have a new assurance and was using a characteristic chorus form for nearly all of his songs.

Said I walked last night, ba-by, feet got soak-ing wet.

Said I walked all night ma-ma

feet got soak-ing wet.___ Said I did-n't

find my wo-man. Ain't stopped walk-in' yet.___

Everything seemed set for them to go on to even more and wider-ranging success. What happened instead was that Fuller was suddenly taken sick.

Fuller had been suffering for some time with a kidney ailment, but it suddenly got worse, and even though he lived for eight more months he didn't record again. According to the death certificate, located by Bastin, Fuller was under a doctor's care from December 12, 1940, but the infection of both the kidneys and bladder had become too advanced. He died on the morning of February 12, 1941, and was buried three days later at Durham's Grove Hill Cemetery. As another young musician who had come into Durham sang:

> They called me to his bedside one morning, and the clock was striking four,
> They called me to his bedside one morning, and the clock was striking four.
> Gonna take my guitar and carry my baby home, I won't stay here no more.

The young singer who got Fuller's guitar was Brownie McGhee and for a time Long tried to have him take Fuller's place.

In the growing and popular blues scene of the late 1930s Fuller's death was not widely noticed. It was a time when a number of singers were very popular, and many younger men were starting to record. Fuller had been very successful, but

168

it seemed that there were a number of artists ready to take his place. For some months it even looked as though Long would be able to replace him with McGhee. Brownie, who had come into Durham from Bristol, Tennessee, where he'd been working with a small instrumental group, had begun recording in the summer of 1940 with Jordan Webb and Robert Young. He did twelve blues for OKeh on August 6 and 7. There was a short session—only two blues—on May 22, 1941, then the next day he did ten more blues, including "Death of Blind Boy Fuller," on OKeh 06265. Many of these releases were labeled "Blind Boy Fuller No. 2," and for a group of religious songs the next day OKeh used the old "Brother George and His Sanctified Singers" name that they'd used for Blind Boy Fuller.

It was a strong effort on Long's part—he even sent Buddy Moss up to New York with McGhee in the fall of 1941, and Moss did his first recordings since 1935. At the same time, however, he sent Sonny Terry, and Brownie and Sonny began playing as a duet in New York, and they never returned to Durham. It had been a young man's scene—Fuller was only thirty-two when he died, and Brownie was twenty-five when he started recording. In December 1941, World War II broke out, and the lives of Durham's younger men became entangled with the war and its disruptions. Within a few months, first the shellac shortage, then the union recording ban, stifled the recording industry, and J.B. Long dropped out of the music business. With Fuller dead, and the most promising of the younger artists, Brownie McGhee, already on his way by himself, the blues scene in Durham suddenly died. The Trice brothers, who had gone with Fuller for his Decca date in 1937, still kept playing, and Richard even recorded again after the war, but they weren't strong enough as musicians or singers to keep the style going by themselves. The last of the important musicians left in the city was Gary Davis.

Davis dropped out of sight toward the end of the thirties; then the welfare agency got in contact with him in 1943. In 1944 he married and was living in Raleigh—then went to New York to visit his wife's children. He was spending more and more time in the North, but in 1948 the welfare agency received a call from the old Durham landlady of Gary's, Mary Hinton. Gary had turned up injured, with ugly leg infections, and in need of help. They arranged medical care for him, and when he was able to travel he went back to New York, to his singing and preaching on the streets, and to the fame and success that was ultimately waiting for him there. With his final departure, except for an occasional itinerant beggar or a little playing by one of the people still left, the streets of Durham fell silent.

19.
To the End
of the Thirties

The sudden expansion of the blues industry, and then the equally sudden dislocation of every aspect of American life during the war years, can be used as a dividing line between the blues of the earlier folk period and the blues styles that developed in the postwar period. But it can only be useful to consider this as a transition period in the blues if it's also kept in mind that it's a blurred and shaky point of division and that many things that may be thought of as characteristic of one period or another were either beginning, or fading, before the end of the Depression and the beginning of the war in Korea.

One of the dominant aspects of the country blues between the mid-twenties and 1940 was the richness and strength of the local rural styles. It's startling to consider the range in a musical form that could include both the gentle, wiry style of Luke Jordan in Virginia and the hard, harsh insistence of Charley Patton in Mississippi. There were the broad regional styles of areas like Texas, the Mississippi Delta, and the Carolinas, and there were styles that were limited to a city and the area around it—such as Memphis and its jug bands and Atlanta with its group centering around its twelve-string guitar players.

The different regional styles of the blues were not only interesting from a musical point of view; they were also interesting for what they suggested of blues origins and of the earlier song forms that became part of the blues. In the rhythms of the blues that Son House recorded in 1930 it was still possible to hear the rhythm of the axe strokes that had marked the work songs his blues had developed from. The dancelike finger-picking rhythms of Blind Blake's Southeast style reflect, just as clearly, a background of house servants and country entertainments. The early field recording units left behind a trove of cultural and musical materials that's so rich we've only begun to sift through its treasures.

But at the same time there were already performers who weren't particularly centered in any area's style. Blind Lemon Jefferson, one of the most successful country bluesmen of the mid-twenties, was clearly in a Texas tradition, and Blind Blake, almost as successful, was just as definitely from a Southeast tradition. But Lonnie Johnson, who was more successful than either of them, could have come from anywhere. He was living in St. Louis when he started recording in 1925, but his style was drawn from so many sources that it would be difficult to point to anything specifically Missourian about it. In the thirties there was an increasing number of artists—especially pianists—who had no clear stylistic home. Many of the most popular artists of the immediate prewar period had this more general identity as commercial blues singers, instead of Mississippi or Tennessee bluesmen. Artists like Peetie Wheatstraw, Roosevelt Sykes, Bumble Bee Slim, Big Bill, Sonny Boy Williamson, and Washboard Sam had absorbed so many influences that they were more like each other than like anything else. The blues, in their terms, was becoming another aspect of the professional music world, and it was that that drew them to the music.

So it isn't entirely useful to think of the prewar period as one dominated completely by regional artists and the instrumental techniques and vocal styles that they shared. There were many artists who were already part of a more general expression of the blues. Also, the war didn't end the regional styles. When small companies began recording in most of the cities of the South in the late forties and early fifties much of what they recorded clearly reflected the continuing local tradition. The music and artists that Trumpet recorded in Jackson, Mississippi, from Willie Love to the second Sonny Boy Williamson, were certainly different from the Texas blues that Bill Quinn recorded in Houston when he put Lightnin' Hopkins in the studio for his Gold Star label.

The war years, then, should probably be thought of as hastening and strengthening tendencies that were already present in the blues, but not as a decisive factor in themselves. The strongest effect the war had on the blues was to change the nature of the blues audience. The demand for labor, and the shifting of thousands of young men from the South, created a large urban black community. Again the shift of black families out of the South that had begun many years before took on the nature of an exodus, both for jobs and for social reasons. The bluesmen lost their country audience, and the blues that developed a few years after the war was a city style, more suited to a nightclub than to a cabin porch or a country juke joint.

At the same time there was a technical innovation—the electric guitar. Suddenly effects were possible that hadn't been before—like the slide technique of Elmore James. With an electric guitar he could sustain tones and emphasize the dramatic elements of what he was doing in a way he couldn't do with an acoustic instrument. The electric guitar also made it possible for a musician to play for a large audience without essentially changing the individualistic or personally expressive aspects of the blues style. It was loud enough to fill a noisy club and, since most of the early amplifiers could also be used with a small microphone to amplify singing or a harmonica, the bluesmen was not a small band.

Five or six years, too, is a long time in popular music, which the blues had certainly become. Between 1940 and 1946 or 1947 there would have been changes in the blues even without the war. The number of artists without clear regional identity had been growing, the people who wanted to hear the blues had been moving more and more to urban areas, and the blues had been moving from a music that was primarily a song form to a dance form for some time. It was the pressures of the war that hurried all these processes, but they were happening by themselves, and the blues was already beginning to reflect the changes.

The story of the blues, then, to the end of the thirties was primarily the story of the country bluesmen developing in their own areas and clarifying and defining their local styles. At the same time the growth of a commercial blues industry centered in Chicago was beginning, and through the thirties the artists active in Chicago, from Big Bill to Memphis Slim, were putting together the commercial elements that were to be utilized by men like Muddy Waters and Howling Wolf when the new generation of bluesmen entered the Chicago scene. The careers of all these artists seem to belong more to a detailed study of Chicago and of the blues that emerged from the postwar years than they do to a study of the local styles that the recording directors found in their wanderings in the twenties.

But all this wealth of music was the background of the postwar blues—then the early rock and roll styles—and finally the pop music of two generations of Americans. The bluesmen from this period probably didn't think of what they were doing in these terms, and even Chicago musicians who watched it happen in the fifties still aren't sure what it was that took place. For most bluesmen the music they play is something that was moving and shaping their society before they were born, and it has gone on taking its place in the larger American society while other styles of music have come and gone around it. It's no wonder that they say "The blues won't never die" or "The blues was here before I came and the blues will be here after I go."

Whatever the future of the blues will be it certainly is part of society's life today, and the roots of the blues that flourished in hundreds of small towns and back-country farms grew so deeply that it's hard to think they could easily be pulled up. The story of the bluesmen is a chronicle of the lives and music of men who were complex and fascinating human beings—and at the same time it's the story of a society and its life and its culture. It's not often in history that a small song has become so deeply entwined with the life of a people. It's this that gives the story of the blues its drama and its excitement.

Appendix: A Note on Some Available Recordings

Thanks to the active reissue programs of a number of independent labels, it's possible to hear a cross section of much of the music discussed in the text of this study. For a general survey of Memphis and its bluesmen probably the most useful albums are the two volumes on Yazoo, *Ten Years in Memphis*, L-1002, and *Frank Stokes' Dream*, L-1008, which includes Frank Stokes, Furry Lewis, Noah Lewis, and Will Weldon, as well as some other singers who recorded in Memphis but weren't part of the musical scene on Beale Street. There is no really satisfactory collection by the Memphis Jug Band available, but the RBF record *The Jug Bands*, RBF 8, includes some early numbers, and the European release *The Memphis Jug Band* on Collectors' Classics has a group of recordings from the thirties sessions. The best selection of John Estes' work is the RBF release, RBF 7, *Sleepy John Estes*; royalties are paid to Estes on sales of this record. Blues Classics has reissued two volumes of Memphis Minnie, *Memphis Minnie* Volumes 1 and 2, and a strong selection of her work is included.

One of the most exciting reissues of Memphis music is Herwin's *Cannon's Jug Stompers*, Herwin 208. Everything recorded by the band is included, as well as Cannon's duets with Blind Blake and the duets with Hosea Woods. The material is presented in chronological order, with excellent sound quality, and there are extensive notes with much new information by Bengt Olsson and transcriptions of the texts. The two-record set is a model of what can be done with reissues of early blues recordings.

The best introduction to Atlanta and its singers continues to be *The Atlanta Blues* on RBF 9, with selections by both Hicks brothers, Peg Leg Howell, Willie McTell, Emery Glen, and Buddy Moss. McTell has now been so extensively reissued that almost everything he did is available on a number of LPs. A selection of earlier work including the Victor sessions has been assembled by Yazoo on L-1005, *Blind Willie McTell, The Early Years*. Biograph LP BLP C14, *Blind Willie McTell, Death Cell Blues*, includes most of the early Columbia and

OKeh material, among the songs the first "Broke Down Engine Blues." Biograph also distributes the McTell session with John Lomax for the Library of Congress that was first issued on Melodean label. The record is MLP 7323, *Blind Willie McTell, October, 1940.* A selection of the songs McTell did at his 1949 Regal sessions has been released by Biograph on BLP 12008, *Blind Willie McTell, 1949, Trying to Get Home,* and another record BLP 12035, *Blind Willie McTell and Memphis Minnie 1949, Love Changin' Blues,* includes the rest of the Regal material, as well as the recordings Memphis Minnie did for the same company at that time.

Thanks to the efforts of a number of blues enthusiasts, among them Simon Napier of *Blues Unlimited* magazine, Atlantic Records has been able to put out the complete McTell sessions supervised by Ahmet Ertegun. It is a very well-produced album with everything McTell did for Atlantic, released and unreleased, including fine versions of both "Broke Down Engine Blues" and "Dyin' Crapshooter's Blues." It is available as SD7224, *Blind Willie McTell, Atlanta Twelve-String.*

Biograph for some time has been involved in an ambitious Blind Blake project, trying to locate and reissue every one of his recordings. Five LPs have been released so far, and they are an excellent cross section of Blake's work, with both his solo blues and his instrumental numbers represented. There are, as well, recordings with other artists, from Viola B. Wilson to Charlie Spand. The first album, BLP 12003, *Blind Blake, 1926-1930, Bootleg Rumdum Blues,* is devoted to solo blues, while the other albums include a variety of styles and accompaniments.

Some of the more interesting work by the coastal singers is scattered through a number of LPs. Willie Walker's two pieces are included in Yazoo's fine *East Coast Blues,* L-1013, which also has William Moore, Bayless Rose, and Carl Martin. The Saydisc album *Blind Boy Fuller on Down* has Julius Daniels, as well as Fuller, Buddy Moss, and the two early blues recordings by Gary Davis. Willie Baker is included in Herwin's *Sic Em Dogs on Me,* Herwin 201. Fuller's work can be found on several LPs, among them RBF 202, *The Rural Blues,* which includes both solo blues and an instrumental rag with Oh Red and Sonny Terry.

index